The Way of PaRC

Welcome.

All content provided in this Intake Booklet is for you to read and keep, except the Signature Page enclosed herein…please sign and submit it with the separate intake form to your therapist/facilitator.

~Dr. Faye

Table of Contents

Essay: Confidentiality & Secrecy

by S. Faye Snyder, PsyD (1995)

Between Therapist and Patient

When you do therapy with me, my trainers, interns, other causal therapists—or any other therapist for that matter—you are entitled to confidentiality. Our licensing requires it. Causal therapists, especially, wish to provide it. Nevertheless, there are limits to the confidentiality I offer. If you have shared with me that you or someone you know has abused, neglected or exploited a dependent adult, an elderly person or a child in your care, or if you have failed to protect a helpless person in your care, we are mandated by my licensing board to report. If I report "against" you, you may be welcome to sit with me in the process. Further, if you lose custody of your child as a result of my report, I pledge to you I will work hard to help you become the best parent you can be, and heal the hurt in your own childhood that led you to abuse or neglect your child. Additionally, I will document your growth for you so earning your child back is effective. Additionally, if you express to me intentions to hurt someone, including yourself, I am mandated to take the steps necessary to protect whoever is at risk.

If you are in couples counseling, I ask you to understand there is a "No Secrets Agreement" that protects both parties. Even though there may be appropriate times for exceptions to this rule, it is an agreement we all make together.

On some occasions I have agreed to keep a secret from a spouse who was in couples counseling. The criteria I would use to keep a confidence confidential is (1) it appears there is too little to be gained by revealing it, and/or (2) it may be more harmful to reveal than helpful.

If you saddle me with a secret, insisting on confidentiality despite our No Secrets Agreement, I may choose to honor your request. If I believe the lack of information puts your partner at a major disadvantage in the relationship (*i.e.*, you are having an affair and intend to continue, knowing this would devastate him or her), then I will have to release myself from treating you as a couple. You would not be investing in the relationship or honoring the No Secrets Agreement, and by continuing with you I would be betraying your partner along with you by keeping your secret. If, in my professional opinion, your secret puts your partner at risk (*i.e.*, a communicable disease), then I will give you a choice between you telling your partner or me.

If you participate in the Relationship Skills Workshop (RSW), you are not guaranteed confidentiality. However, all members of the group in which you belong will have been asked to honor confidentiality. They will be allowed to discuss their experiences in the workshop with others, but they are simply not allowed to reveal names, and if they do so, they agree to hear out the group's disappointment, member by member. You will not be allowed to saddle another member of the group with a secret they cannot share with the group, if it pertains to the group process. Revealing information about a member of the group to the public lacks ethics; if you do so, you may be exiled from the group, and from PaRC altogether.

Nevertheless, one of the most important lessons you will learn from RSW is: There is no need for secrecy in an environment where <u>judgment is not tolerated</u>. When you live an open life you are expected to take responsibility for your words, choices and actions. You will learn how to live your life in integrity and as free of judgment as possible, with the skills to defend against the judgement of others. You will also learn better assessment skills so you can assess the ethics and mental health of potential partners and friends before you get in too deep.

There is a time for secrecy. For example, if the truth will cause harm to an innocent person, it is moral and ethical to keep a secret and unethical to tell anyone who would expose the party needing such protection. If you are hiding Jews in your attic to protect them from Nazis, you must vigilantly maintain your secret.

If I am treating someone for kleptomania, it is important she have the safety of confidentiality. She will need to freely discuss all her drives to steal in order to heal. In this case secrecy will lead to an open and healthy lifestyle someday. Confidentiality is necessary to get her there. This would be true of any destructive or self-destructive behavior held secret. I would also need to keep a bank heist or even murder a secret if I am treating someone who has no further plans to kill and wants treatment to ensure he or she will not kill again. Confidentiality is necessary to do this work.

<u>**Avoiding Karma**</u>

While it is incumbent upon your therapist to keep your private sessions confidential, this therapist does not want you to consider confidentiality an approval of secrecy as an ethic or a lifestyle.

As a therapist and a person who places a strong value on ethics, I believe we should not be allowed to get away with dishonorable behavior. That does not mean I have a thirst to punish or to see punishment take place. I have not. As a matter of fact, I consider the drive to judge and punish a possible symptom of an illness. I believe reality provides plenty of natural consequences that are wonderfully configured to force us naturally to self-correct. However, when a dependent person is at risk, it is incumbent upon us to tell.

In other cases secrecy allows us to be someone we are not. Living in secrecy protects us from the natural consequences of our behavior and enables us to continue behaving in ways that are damaging to ourselves, our relationships, and to others. It deprives us of an authentic life.

<u>**Unburdening without Consequences**</u>

Secrecy is often designed to allow someone to unburden their heavy conscience while avoiding the natural consequences of their misdeed. Often the notion of loyalty is coupled with secrecy to further protect someone from the consequences of their actions. The secret may be shared to lighten the load. In this way intimacy is launched and loyalty is consecrated with a "promise-not-to-tell" and then this pact is finalized by a threat of emotional blackmail. Nevertheless, the 'holder' of this secret now has to find someone else upon whom she can unburden her load.

As much as natural consequences tend to ultimately teach us lessons for bad choices, when that behavior is actually a crime or puts weaker people in jeopardy, secrecy is unethical and constitutes conspiracy. I say this harshly because there is a time to tell. For example, if an adult is molesting a child and swears another adult to secrecy, keeping that secret implicates the secret keeper as a co-conspirator. That child and future children would be protected were the secret out. Any conspiracy to protect a criminal act against helpless or dependent persons is wrong, if not evil. Further, where there is the capacity for one criminal act there is a probability of past and future ones, unless the perpetrator is exposed, identified and treated, if possible.

A sin worse than abuse is repression. Repression deprives a victim of the opportunity to recover. This is classically when the victim herself is asked or told not to tell by her offender or her offender's supporters. She has been asked to put her offender's wishes above her own needs. Most of these clients have complied for some period of time. In these cases, the client was not only the victim, but now she has been forbidden to work through her traumatic experience in deference to someone who doesn't deserve such a sacrifice. The injury is now compounded since the victim has been further violated by the request she keep the improper secret herself, to protect her offender.

Ironically, the victim often thinks protecting their offender has some nobility to it. I am proposing that protecting abusive people is unethical. No matter how innocent one is of injuring others, it is unethical not to report abuse of an innocent person, even if that person is yourself.

Healers are in a parental and care giving role with weaker or dependent persons. I have known situations in which the doctor was "seduced" by a patient, and succumbed, which is as outrageous as a parent blaming his child for seducing her. However, the person who has the power to determine events, such as the therapist/doctor/counselor/clergy is always the responsible party, just as the parent or adult is always the responsible party. Some therapists who have exploited their client(s) actually blame the weaker party for seducing them, even though she took the training for her profession to include ethics, agreed to the licensing requirements and now holds the position of authority. She becomes honor-bound to provide a healthy and moral compass. When one becomes an authority, the copout that the child or the patient "made me do it," is inexcusable. The child is still in training, and the patient is a patient because she does not yet know how to represent herself and is often still predisposed to sacrifice her own needs for those of parents or authority figures. She may have wrongly learned that to ingratiate herself to someone in authority makes her safer or more valuable. This is especially the case when she is the weaker party and so may be prone to act out childhood experiences in the context of treatment.

Mental health is always threatened by secrecy of this magnitude and cannot survive bad ethics. Saddling a child or a patient with a secret inflicts further injury by truncating the opportunity to heal and rebound. The capacity to work through childhood issues such as sexual abuse, addiction, parental weakness, unethical role modeling, exploitation, parentification (taking care of the parent) and family secrets, has now been compromised.

The client or patient now has been forced into carrying a secret to protect her therapist, parent, religious leader, mate or boss against her own interests.

All of this is to say our mental health and that of those around us depends upon whistleblowers. Whistleblowers are the guardians of society, and secret keepers (even the victims) are our weakest link. I am a mandated reporter against dependent abuse and victims of sexual exploitation. Those of us in the helping professions are the definitive reporters. However, when it comes to sexual relations between a therapist and a client, unfortunately we cannot report for you. All of us need you to step up when the time comes. Doing so will promote your mental health.

Protecting a False Image

Sometimes secrecy protects a false image. A healthy life is one where truth can be put on the table, and life can be lived in the open. In other words, if you don't want anyone to know you're an alcoholic, you need to give up drinking. If you don't want anyone to know you're a kleptomaniac, you need to give up stealing. If you don't want someone to know you're unfaithful to your mate, be faithful, or get a divorce. Therapy will help you get to the drives or choices that led to your infidelity, but it should also look at the values that allowed you to practice ignoble behavior for so long. Most likely you will identify poor role modeling gone unchecked.

If you have a husband who will lie to the boss for you when you have a hangover, you need to free him from lying for you. When nature becomes our natural adviser, we do our best growing. If you were in couples counseling, I might personally advise your mate to stop protecting you. I'd suggest you call for yourself and perhaps say, "George, I'm going to either come into work with a hangover or I'm going right now to find an AA meeting, which do you prefer? Odds are, you will not be fired. Living life "out of the truth" only gets you in deeper. Living life in the truth gets you stronger faster, and earns you real respect to replace the false respect you have been seeking.

Avoiding Rejection

Lives lived in fear someone will learn a truth then reject you are often liberated in the process of good therapy. Sometimes it starts with telling the therapist your secret and ends with you telling the truth and dealing with the fallout. Sometimes the fallout turns out to be nothing after all. Sometimes the fallout forces you to self-correct and grow. Sometimes the fallout is compassion you have carried so much for so long for so little reason. Sometimes the fallout is to discover most of us have pasts, and when you shared yours they were inspired to share theirs in return. Sometimes we discover our own character and the true character of others when we release a secret. Sometimes it is revealed to us with whom we should be in a relationship and whom we should let go. Sometimes we learn what we need to do to make amends. Sometimes we simply discover the intimacy of sharing without burdening the other with a secret. Most of us develop a taste for relationships that include forgiveness for the sake of growth.

Commiserating with Denial

Many of us hustle others to hear the "truth" we want to hear. Once I was a matchmaker for a dating business. The sales department, either having no scruples or no vision, sold a package to a woman who was about 5'5" tall and weighed about 300 pounds. I could not provide a date for her without deceiving other paying clients. I finally decided to confront her with the truth.

"Delilah" (name changed), I said, "You have so many wonderful traits. There must be many people who would love to know you. I could match you up with some people you might enjoy, except for one problem…" I paused at this point. I always pause at this point because if I'm about to tell someone something they'd rather not hear, I prefer it be their choice. Hopefully they will take this opportunity to own the problem aloud.

"What's that?" Delilah asked on time.

"Your weight," I responded, a bit disappointed she didn't seize the moment of truth. "Most people would have difficulty with your weight."

"What's wrong with my weight?!" she demanded. I was caught by surprise. I didn't expect this because I was sure she knew what I meant. I decided to follow with an estimate of how many pounds she might be over weight, and I proposed she was at about double what a healthy weight would be for her. Before I could say, "You're about double a healthy weight," she spoke again.

"There is nothing wrong with my weight. I don't know anybody who thinks there is anything wrong with my weight."

"Well, I'll tell you what," I suggested. "You ask ten people among your family and friends what they think, and then we'll talk again."

Delilah called me the next day. She had spoken to ten people from her family and friend group and, additionally, ten strangers in front of Ralph's grocery store. They had all agreed with her there is nothing wrong with her weight! I can picture it now. I can see an obese woman asking strangers in front of Ralph's, "Is there anything wrong with my weight?"

"No," they'd say, passing by her, not wanting to get into it, and getting on with their business.

The lesson is this: If asked the right way, we can get just about anyone to agree with us about nearly anything. That's how denial can work for so long. How you ask the question telegraphs how honest an answer you seek.

Avoiding Rudeness

Some people raised in dishonesty believe you're supposed to lie to protect other's feelings. One woman told me she confronted her mother about how she'd never been told the truth about things growing up and how every conversation they'd had was superficial. Nobody was allowed to tell the truth about their feelings, and they couldn't even tell the truth to each other about the littlest things. Her mother replied, "That's a social skill, honey. You're not supposed to tell people the truth. It hurts people's feelings." The woman asked her mother back, "Do you have any idea how much it's hurt me all these years to never have a real conversation with you and to never know how you really felt about me or what you really thought? Do you really believe I can't handle a little pain now and then in order to know what the truth is?"

Some of us learn in early childhood, "If you don't have anything nice to say, don't say it." We learn to be good little positive thinkers for our parent's sake. Some of us even learn in infancy not to cry because it upsets our parents too much. As a matter of fact, hiding negative feelings becomes an ingrained and primitive talent that is predicated on survival, and if anyone moves to challenge our airs we may reflexively snap back like a cornered dog. Hiding negative feelings leads to an inauthentic personality, which conceals a lifetime's worth of buried fear, hurt and anger. Having become so fake, we secretly believe way down inside we are not good, that we are, in fact, frauds for good cause. We may actually believe if we ever explore the truth of who we are, it will be discovered we are inherently bad or unlovable. So at our core, underneath all our upbeat attempts to be positive, we may be hiding a deep depression for our parents' sake. To heal this drive to be deceptive about ourselves lest people judge us, we have to decide whether or not we are willing to secretly betray our parents in the confidentiality of therapy so we can finally be free to be ourselve—our real selves.

Sometimes we worry that we shouldn't express feelings, or that truthful information will make our parents uncomfortable about themselves or cause them to feel betrayed by us.

So much concern for the feelings of others turns out to be a fear the other person will get mad at us. We're really worried for ourselves. We don't like to feel someone's negative feelings, especially if they're directed at us. Perhaps we don't know what to do. Are we supposed to fend it off, defend, or avoid it? No. We really are simply supposed to allow the other person to express themselves, if only briefly. It won't hurt us. We would do well to say, "I'm so glad you could tell me how you feel." Perhaps we can say, "Thank you for your honesty. I will consider what you have said." Most of us don't realize it simply won't hurt and we *can* handle it. Handling it earns us respect and teaches others as well as ourselves to grow.

Hiding to Avoid Authenticity

So much deception and secrecy is done in order to appear good. If people only knew how much those from whom they are hiding are also hiding, more of us would stop pretending in life and start living for real.

If you bring your spouse into therapy, you must understand and agree to keep no secrets. That means if I am forced to keep marriage-related matters secret, I may have to terminate work with you to avoid betrayal of your spouse, when I have information he deserves to know. This is perhaps the only way a couples therapist can remain ethical. Some people have been raised in a mire of deception and think nothing of asking professional secret keepers to join them. Nevertheless, when one understands by keeping a secret for Millie, I am betraying the mental health of Nick, one can see my only alternatives are to betray confidentiality (not an option), to insist Millie either reveal her secret or quit her betrayal, or to terminate therapy. Of course, the next therapist and any who follow will also have the same dilemma.

Thus, good therapists do not keep confidentiality comfortably at all times. If we had no problem with secrecy, no matter what the secret, and if we believed in a secrecy ethic, then we might be *enablers* of your pathology. It is not therapeutic to contribute to protecting your dysfunctional fears. A good therapist may push you to tell the truth or to even expose your unhealthy choices or habits. A good therapist may encourage you to share a burden with someone. A good therapist may ask you to take a look at your worst fears and to plan for various possibilities that might come with disclosures. A relationship group or group therapy is a safe place to begin, as long as the therapist can assure your safety and protection from misguided or mean-spirited feedback. Look for a group that has rules against judging others within the group and where understanding others in the room is the ultimate goal. In this case a therapist can evaluate and help you correct your coping mechanisms too.

This does not mean matters irrelevent to the health of the marriage must be brought out. Sometimes it is important to determine what is relevant and necessary to communicate as well as what is irrelevant and unnecessary to say. For example, both parties *may need* to put on the table whether or not they had consenting sex with other adults before their marriage, but may not need to discuss with whom or how much, unless it's truly relevant. If a mate was sexually abused in childhood and has not been treated for that abuse, it might be important material to share with a prospective mate or a spouse with whom sexual intimacy issues have developed. If the sexual abuse has been treated, it may not be relevant material to bring up. On the other hand, part of treating sexual abuse is removing the secrecy and repression ethic from the trauma. Part of treating sexual abuse is realizing you are not to blame and sharing your pain with others who will give you support and understanding. Another part of healing sexual abuse is giving up the role of victim and finding the courage to make healthy choices and put unhealthy choices under scrutiny. Actually, I have never met a treated victim of sexual abuse who needed to continue their secrecy.

Secrecy is sometimes appropriate, but for the most part, a person who lives in secrets and keeps secrets from those with whom he frequently interacts is handicapping his relationships and sacrificing his authenticity. Living an inauthentic life is painful and unfulfilling. Living an authentic life is rewarding.

Between Therapists

Please understand I agree confidentiality is an essential context for healing. My issue is there is something pathological about the way some therapists wear it and represent it. I see therapists telegraphing the importance of keeping secrets and the patient picks up on it. It can be an unhealthy message when we should be encouraging clients to live life without the need for secrets.

Perhaps it's my imagination, but I keep running across evidence that confidentiality can become a life-style for therapists, even out of the frame, as well as a cover for our own inadequacies in the frame. Sometimes it appears confidentiality has turned into a mandated blind spot. Other times it appears those parts of us still in denial are attracted to confidentiality and wear it as a validating cover. At this point in time, I dare say confidentiality is more important to therapists than it is to clients, although I believe it should be defended and protected for those clients who really need it.

Narcissism seems to lie at the core of the excessive protection of confidentiality. Some of us become therapists to help others in order to get our identity needs met. When a young child learns he has to disguise his true feelings and observations to protect his parents' feelings, lack of authenticity is born as a personality disorder. The child learns to bury his pain and anger for his parents' sake and "put on a happy face." He learns "if you can't say anything nice, don't say anything at all." He learns he must be a positive mirror for his parents—and ultimately for the world—and he should "forgive and forget" and "let the past be the past." He learns sometimes it's not polite to tell the truth or some truths should not be told, or even that most people can't handle the truth, especially parents and patients. Some grow up with this ethic. Others are revolted by the weakness of people and become chronically contemptuous of other people and honesty. Any of these can be maintained in the psychotherapeutic arena under the guise of confidentiality. Incompetence can be preserved the same way.

The untreated narcissistic therapist may still object to any material that "blames the parents" and could be inclined to help the patient reframe his or her anger away from the parent, a la behavioral theory, or even toward the self, a la internal drive theory. A cognitive theorist may focus on positively thinking one's way out of a depression rather than explore the acting out so as to uncover the scary original wounds. A behavioral theorist might look at a child who's bouncing off the walls from repressing untold anger, hurt and fear for their parents, and diagnose them with ADHD. They might then refer the child for medication without even assessing the family system. The child will meet with a psychiatrist who will prescribe Ritalin or the like, and return to a behaviorist while the parents will learn more modern state-of-the-art techniques for controlling and repressing the child.

All the contemporary variations on treating "bad seeds" rather than original wounds and their concomitant repressed feelings lead to a need for confidentiality, a la the confessional. Rather than learning to identify acting out as clear clues and communicators of original injury, therapists often rush to modify the behavior while colluding to keep the ugly secrets. In this way we don't have to unearth the ugly emotions underlying the behavior. In this way we don't have to presuppose that behind the ugly behavior is an innocent child, perhaps now grown, and a damaged, untreated parent.

Sometimes—not often—a high regard for secrecy is imperative. Sometimes what is more important is that the client who requires secrecy has confidence their therapist is capable of protecting his or her privacy. Sometimes the secret needs to be aired so it can die in the therapist's office. Sometimes the client needs to feel safe enough to open up, and the only place they can do that is in therapy. Ultimately, however, a client is not healed if they leave therapy still believing in privacy and secrecy as a lifestyle.

When therapists look at confidentiality as more than privacy, they possibly telegraph shame to the patient. We need to be careful never to allow confidentiality to turn into a cloak for client shame or therapist inadequacies. We need to be certain we don't let the somewhat unnaturalness of the frame turn into a feeling that stigmatizes the client or casts her as an inferior person in our ambiance of mystified boundaries and superiority and our aura of aloofness and perfect appropriateness.

When the therapist looks at their patient as an innocent victim who only learned to cope in ways that would protect their parents, they don't see the need for confidentiality or secrecy quite so clearly. The therapist is just trying to remove arrows from their patient's soul by listening to that which can finally be said. Confidentiality should usually be seen as a private sanctuary for working through forbidden thoughts and urges. As you can tell by this document, my clients are encouraged to be open about their lives, and they continue to surprise and delight me with their openness and relief.

The trouble with confidentiality and narcissism is they can conspire together in an iatrogenic sort of way to perpetuate pathology. There are certain myths they tend to authenticate:

- One should leave the therapy office feeling good.
- I am to blame (perhaps bad) for my mental illness (not my parents).
- Confidentiality implies I should keep my innermost self a secret.
- Secrecy is healthy and appropriate.
- Therapists should help me keep my secrets.
- One should not express anger or pain, rather should act nice in the real world, even if they don't feel it.
- Pain should be avoided because it's hard for other people to take, even therapists.
- Therapy is about learning to mask the badness inside and feeling better, or learning to be happy like everybody else (is acting).
- My life is nobody else's business but mine.
- What I'm discussing *should* be a secret.
- Therapists are not only supposed to lack judgment, but they should be permissive and invested in ethical behavior.

Case Studies

Mary decided to try therapy again because she was still lonely and rather afraid of people and relationships. When her new therapist discussed participation in a relationship skills group as part of her treatment, she declined because too many people would know her business. When this therapist suggested she needed to work on her fear of intimacy, she expressed surprised because her last therapist had told her, "You certainly have a right to your privacy."

This therapist asked Mary what kinds of things she would be afraid people would find out that she didn't want anyone to know. She thought for a while and finally said, "It's not about anything in particular, I'm just afraid people will judge me if they know me."

"Have you avoided relationships because you fear judgment? Have you thought *to be known is to be judged?*" Mary thought a minute and answered "yes."

"Perhaps you need to learn how to respond to someone's judgments, and perhaps you need to learn how to avoid relationships with judgmental people, and finally, perhaps you could learn to give up being so judgmental yourself. You need to know by what criteria one should decide who is safe for the long-term relationship and who is worthy of your openness."

Judy's mother died when she was a young child. She still seemed wounded and vulnerable. She never got over it and entered therapy as a young woman. Her therapist was a woman and they worked together for years. Judy fell in love and became engaged. She asked her therapist if she would come to the wedding.

Judy's therapist told her something like this (and you've heard it before yourself): "Your confidentiality should be guarded at all costs. It wouldn't be safe. This is what boundaries are for. You need to be protected at your wedding from awkward moments that come with socializing." Judy still didn't understand why it wouldn't be safe to invite her therapist to her wedding. Her therapist further explained maybe Judy might notice her talking to one of her friends. Maybe the friend might ask how she knew Judy. Maybe she might accidentally reveal their therapeutic relationship by being avoidant or maybe Judy would be wondering what her therapist was saying about her to other people.

I cannot be certain this is what her therapist said to her, but I do know this is what Judy at least inferred from what she said. If the therapist gave her the impression she could not control what she might say, I believe that was a mistake. This is a person who has been trying to learn to trust. She needs the skills to know how to tell if a person is trustworthy and what to say or do when they fail to act trustworthy. If her own therapist can't control what she might say about Judy, who can she trust? Her own therapist does not appreciate her own reasons for not going to the wedding. She is simply mimicking something she was taught was ethical. She failed to see therapy is a corrective emotional experience and she could fill in the role of Judy's mother at Judy's wedding. Judy had suffered the profound loss of her mother as a child. It would have been meaningful for her therapist to be there. It might even have made Judy proud. She could have gone to the wedding but not the reception. Judy was not worried about confidentiality. She was not worried about what her therapist might say until her therapist told her she should worry about it. Judy suffered another loss, a symbolic loss of her mother again.

Josephine, a social worker, and Dr. Mario, a psychiatrist, taught analytic theory to graduate students in the field of psychology. They taught the material together and had a practice together too. They had different last names, so most of us didn't think at first they were married. At one point, a discussion on television talk shows developed, and they each expressed their disgust that people would open their lives up in public like that.

The last day of class, a student asked if they were married. One of them responded, while the other remained silent, "Why would you want to know that?"

Confidentiality had become a lifestyle, or perhaps they were predisposed and attracted to the profession's lifestyle of confidentiality. They had become people who lacked spontaneity and openness, so much so they verged on dishonesty and deception.

When the Caller I.D. gadgets came out, I received a mailer from one of the officers of a professional organization of therapists to which I belong. She was sounding the alarm against caller ID and suggested therapists get their numbers blocked and advise all their clients to get their numbers blocked as well. She went on to say it's part of our profession to recognize areas in which confidentiality might be violated, and technology has brought a new threat to privacy. As I thought about it, I wondered, except for annoying solicitations, whom might I call who I wouldn't want to know who I am? I wondered what kind of person would make calls to me not wanting me to know their identity? Further, I wondered why I should not know who is calling me? Finally, I wondered if our mandate to confidentiality might make some of us paranoid or if any of us might even have taken up this profession to insulate ourselves from personal responsibility? I threw it in the trash, and I have regretted it since, as I'd love to quote it exactly.

Once, I had a famous client sitting in my reception room waiting with a few others for the rest of her group to arrive. An unknown face was waiting there as well. My *very* famous student inquired enthusiastically if he was going to be a new member of group. A few days later I got an irate call from my landlord regarding my patients violating the confidentiality of other patients by talking to them in the waiting room. I am guessing it was the therapist, not the patient, who was upset, so upset as to not be clear there is no confidentiality promised in the waiting room between patients. It's up to them to set their own boundaries. I did, however, ask the members of my group not to talk to other people's clients in the waiting room. What a shame.

On one occasion, we were taping the parenting class. I had a very large office, the largest in the suite to accommodate such classes. However, I had to share the waiting room and a common area, which led to five doors and offices. Since a number of my students were arriving, I had left the door open for a few minutes. One of the therapists shielded his client with his coat as he was leaving. He complained having the door open for my group to come in was a violation of confidentiality for his clients. I wondered if I were just allowing one client to come into my office at the same time his client was coming or leaving, would he have still felt it necessary to shield his client with his coat.

When I was in graduate school I was taking a class, Supervision II. Our professor told each of us to bring in a dialogue from one of our sessions. We could tape record it or bring in a transcript. In this class of fourteen students, every student reported on their case study with a transcript. Each of them said they didn't have any clients who agreed to being recorded. Remarkably, all of my clients had agreed to taping. All of them were even open to being video taped as well. I brought in a videotape.

The next semester in Supervision III, we were given the same assignment again. I asked permission to bring one of my clients, and my professor was delighted. The response from other students was retentive, except for one woman who brought in a tape recording. She was an excellent student who had evidenced all along that she really grasped the work of therapy. I was not surprised she brought in a tape recording. It supported my unfolding hypothesis that confidentiality may be more for the therapist than the patient.

I had an intern once who intervened every time I gave a member of my relationship skills group honest feedback. It was as if she leapt between me and my student to protect him or her. She would follow up with something reassuring or, at times even attempted to counter the information I had given. She feared honesty. She left my internship because she "disagreed."

Once I had occasion to return to therapy for myself. It was shortly after Susan Forward had her license suspended for telling the police and the public how frightened Nicole Simpson had been of her ex-husband.

I told my therapist I didn't want confidentiality. As a matter of fact, I told her, "if anyone calls asking about how my therapy is going, you tell them." I presented her with a written release. "I can't do that," she told me. "Is that for you or for me?" I asked. "For you," she answered. "In that case," I said, "I won't be back." She held her position, and I did too.

Several years later, I became a member of the Santa Monica Zen Center, which entitled me to Daisan (private interview) with Yoshin, Sensei. I began by requesting he not maintain confidentiality for me, if he ever had any information based on our talks that would clear things up for anyone. "I can't do that," he told me. "Is that for you or for me?" I asked. "That's for me," he answered. I was glad to stay.

I have a new therapist I see now regarding time and financial issues and strategies, especially with Prop. 10 funds becoming available to those who know how to pursue them. She was referred to me by a colleague. I informed her I would be happy for her to share any information regarding my work with my colleague, and I had no reciprocal hopes regarding her breaking confidentiality for my colleague. I told her I didn't want confidentiality unless I shared anything regarding a client or regarding my husband, who I considered entitled to confidentiality. I gave her my statement in writing. She did not say anything. Rather, she accepted the document. I stayed.

I had a client who was a retired therapist. Janet came to see me because her daughter told her if she didn't learn to be more open, they could never have a real relationship. Her daughter complained her mother had been closed to her throughout her entire childhood. I asked my client to go home and share her insights with her daughter as they came up. This forced my client into an internal dialogue that amounted to an assumption she thought she could do the therapy in private, keeping the material she unearthed secret, and then be more open with her daughter. On her first day in group, I expressed openly to her and in front of my other students, I felt a little insecure having a therapist in the group and I hoped if she had any issues with me about how I work she would agree to bring them up to me. She was surprised I would disclose such a vulnerable feeling in front of her and the others. She noticed I had modeled openness safely. As a matter of fact, she said, it touched her. She realized her training had reinforced a secrecy ethic she had learned in childhood.

I had a student in my relationship skills workshop whose sister was a psychologist. Her sister wanted my license number because she thought there was something wrong with a therapist who allowed friends to join the same group. (As a matter of fact, I encourage my students to bring relatives and friends and anyone with whom they would like to develop the skills of open communication.) My student's therapist-sister was mortified each student's right to privacy and confidentiality was being violated, by admitting them to the same group as their dear and close friends. This was a sister with whom my able student had a lifetime of difficulty communicating. Her biggest issue with her sister was her ongoing need to preserve her identity as the superior sister.

At a recent dinner party I attended, one of the guests asked, "If given the choice between truth and goodness (Talk Show Host Dennis Praeger's reported philosophical dilemma for Thanksgiving '96), should one go with goodness?" The other therapist at the table blurted out "You wouldn't want to tell a dying person they were dying, would you?" I responded, "If I were dying, I would want to know." I did not add what I was thinking, "And if I lived long enough, I might want to sue you for not telling me the truth."

I cannot help but think (perhaps because I *am* a therapist) such a sharp and sudden rejection of "truth" as opposed to "good," followed by an abrupt leaving of the table, is a sign a person could be uncomfortable with the negative feelings that can come with truth, because they have not yet shed the role of positive mirror for their own parents, and because they have not faced their own buried pain out of loyalty to their parents. I believe if you cannot do it for yourself, you cannot lead another to do it. I believe our field is abundant with internal drive theorists and behaviorists who refuse to contemplate the contents of the "black box" because they have not done their own work yet. Perhaps this makes them too compatible with confidentiality. If you are afraid to face buried hurt, fear and anger left over from childhood, you must be repressed or closed, inauthentic, somewhat incompetent, or perhaps even dishonest. If you do not have a deep and abiding reverence for the truth, you may not be a good role model. It would seem to me you'd have to hold sacred a treasured place in your heart for secrecy and deception. Hiding out in the frame might suit you just fine, especially that part about confidentiality, but if this is what you are doing, you are defrauding your patients.

Playing "good" could be like playing God. It reminds me of the adage, "If you give a person a fish they can eat for a day. If you teach them how to fish, they can eat for a lifetime." I'm inclined to think if you do *good* for a person you make them weak. If you tell them the truth with good intentions, they may become strong by choice. When the good person is gone, the client may return to secrecy. When you reveal truth, its effects are longer lasting and more abundant.

In Conclusion

I believe there is very little truth that cannot be told. I believe if you use skills and kindness, you can reduce pain in the long run by telling the truth sooner than later. I do not believe truth leads to blame. When it does, you have identified a person with whom it is not safe to be in a relationship. I believe truth simply reveals cause and effect. I believe truth is an opportunity to heal, as well as bring wisdom.

On the occasion when someone has not been worthy of my confidence, I would relegate them to the "unsafe" category. I might give them a chance to recover first, by saying, "Wow! I just trusted you and you judged me." I drop them, unless they self-reflect.

I'd rather have as much truth as I can get it. So much evil is done via deception. Truth exposes evil, which is often cloaked in good. While good depends upon personalities and is often the cloak of deception, truth as a system would become a place where evil and deception could not hide, a working goal of healing.

Essay: The No-Blame Contract

by S. Faye Snyder, PsyD

Of all my work, I find the most difficult concept to teach is NO BLAMING. I have often seen those who initially nod in agreement later will be the ones to assert it doesn't apply to them or their circumstances.

Some people simply cannot comprehend life without blaming. They have always thought in terms of innocence and blame. They have not yet grasped or been shown the notion of personal responsibility and self-reflection as a tool to redirect the course of their lives toward healthier and happier results. Self-reflection is what other people need to do. Furthermore, when I try to interrupt the blame process, I sometimes find I become the target. It's a difficult concept to teach. I hope if I lay this out in this way, I may have a shot at proving to my beloved students I am not singling them out, and I do actually understand the problem.

One thing I want my clients to get up front is I do not believe it is the responsibility of a therapist to accept blame for not tolerating blame. I don't tolerate being blamed, and that is a model for you, the student, as well. It is as excruciating for me as for anyone, and I don't believe tolerating blame is the right thing to do. It is unnatural. My intolerance of blame is healthy. Unnatural is to stay and fight or to submit. So, this is my disclaimer. I do not tolerate blame. I can be expected to abruptly terminate therapy if the client begins to blame me for my intolerance, for reacting negatively or for "yelling" in order to protect their right to blame without feeling "judged" for it. I do raise my voice when someone is defying me as their teacher. I can get stern. In a way I am the real parent. A real parent who is teaching ethics and values will not tolerate blaming behavior. There are consequences, even if it is rebuke. A good parent will forgive instantly, after succeeding at stopping the blaming. A good parent can move on instantly. I can do that easily.

I generally don't yell, but when I do it's a natural consequence to blaming. When people blame it is just about intolerable to be on the other end, and the feeling of not being heard or understood tends to cause someone to want to speak louder, take a stand or raise their voice. Often it is the unrelenting blamer who yells and insists the other, especially the therapist, not raise her voice or frown or wince or give any "disrespectful" feedback for what this therapist considers very bad behavior. Blaming clients hide behind a shield of hypocrisy wherein they demand others respect them when they don't respect others.

If someone won't stop, then I "make an arrest." I demand the person stop blaming. If they won't, then we have to regretfully terminate the relationship, perhaps something the blamer should have done themselves in life rather than stay in an intolerable situation.

The following is a tool for great change, but it must be fully embraced, as the concepts within, however plainly written, are Greek to the uninitiated. If you are humble and seriously looking over the mistakes you have made in your past relationships, you are entitled to be treated with total reverence by your therapist or your listener. If this does not happen, you may need to request it because you and I both know this is delicate work and you will be feeling fragile. But you must also know when you slip into 12 o'clock or into blame-consciousness, the respect you earned will disappear, and you may even be treated as a criminal until you fall back to that precious, humble state of learning, re-building and re-creating yourself wherein I get to be your co-creator.

Childhood

Please know: a review of our childhoods and what we learned when we were young is not about blaming parents. When one understands we learn our ways in childhood, we realize our parents learned their ways in their childhoods. It then becomes possible to identify our injuries, self-correct and forgive our parents. We all have mirror neurons, which record the way we are treated and reference these recordings for our reflexive behaviors toward others.

As Gabor Mate, MD, who specializes in addictive behavior, including the origins of addictive behavior, has said: We are born with two primary needs or drives. One is to be loved and to love in return. The other is to become authentic. Most of us sell off our need to be authentic in order to be loved. Thus, our development becomes stuck.

When we have childhood injuries and are not free to get help or express our pain to our misunderstanding parent(s), we repress those feelings and lose our authenticity. When we lose our authenticity, we begin to live "underground," keeping our true feelings and thoughts to ourselves. We become unknowable. A child who is already underground when they become molested may be driven to perpetrate, and when a child is free to tell his or her story of injury, they will likely heal. Those of us who protect our parents at all cost tend to scapegoat others instead of identifying the injury and releasing it with a true story and the emotions that come with it.

Alcoholics Anonymous holds "If it's hysterical, it's historical." That means if we don't identify our injuries, expressing them out of our bodies in an unmailed letter, by doing some rage work at an empty chair or simply telling a therapist or dear friend and receiving empathy, we won't heal.

Some people were raised in environments wherein their parents judged and blamed them. Others were raised witnessing their parents judge and blame others. Others were raised in an environment where there was no perceptible bar, and the child could do anything, such that when they behaved unethically, they learned to deflect and blame. Some blame by playing the role of the frightened victim. Others just insist they are being treated wrongly and demand respect no matter how they act. They have no idea respect is earned. Trust is earned. Anyone who gets close to them will need to feel safe to make mistakes and to even be selfish. We are born to be selfish, or self-representing. We learn to think of ourselves and our survival first, until someone teaches us self-sacrifice and empathy by modeling them.

Some of us grew up in environments where healthy interaction skills were not practiced. We grew up where responsibility for how we were doing and how we felt was always on others, usually parents in power who were blaming us or even parents who inoculated us from responsibility by rescuing us at every turn. We may have grown up believing accepting personal responsibility meant accepting blame. Many of us have spent our whole childhood and adult lives ducking blame. Many become professional victims in the process. Others become superior acting, judgmental narcissists. Thus, we enter into our adult lives on the offense to avoid blame. We believe if or since we are not to blame, the other guy obviously is.

When a Child Becomes an Adult

Our own unhealed past determines how we treat people. While products of a blame ethic, we actually blame reflexively. While we suffered from being blamed and suffer now because we have not self-reflected, we don't imagine such suffering in the other person we blame. While we hate being blamed, we don't understand the other person's reaction to feeling blamed. We have one-way streets. We are hypocritical. We don't see cause and effect. We don't see the elements in the situation. Rather, we react and defend our exclusive right to react, while we add up all our righteous reasons. We tend to look at all these painful exchanges as coming from the other person, exclusively, without any consideration of what was our part. Our part incudes expectations from them to be regardful and loyal no matter how we treat them. We then have projections of our fears of what they will do to us and how we are there to guarantee ourselves no one will ever hurt us again. In this way, we create our own self-fulfilling prophesy.

Blame comes from pain. The illusion is, "If I am in pain, someone else created my pain." The truth is, "The way I interpret the behavior of others creates my pain." Further, the way I interpret pain comes from my childhood. I learned how to interpret this pain of being disrespected and misunderstood and devalued from the way I saw my parents and caregivers treat each other, as well as the way they treated me. We bring that very pain from childhood to our adult relationships and then transfer insulting past experiences along with the pent-up pain to our adult intimate relationships.

Of course, there are real experiences in adulthood of being insulted and injured, but we have not recognized how those experiences are born of the other person's past that were there when we met them. For numerous reasons we were perhaps poor at vetting the people with whom we formed intimate relationships. We have had our own history of choosing relationships for our own self-absorbed reasons. We have chosen poorly, but we blame the other person for who they turned out to be while they were with us, as if they should have magically become safe once they chose to be with us. We tend to look at how they act as having nothing to do with their past or with us. The way they are, we think, is who they are, unless we can fix them, blame them and protest enough to change them, thereby making them pay for how they have treated us. This way of thinking lacks self-reflection, insight and maturity.

How Blamers Create Relationships

Typically, blamers or judgers only have two criteria to evaluate candidates for a future relationship: they see the other person either likes them or they don't. These two choices lead to a dance of mutual admiration or mutual dislike. The other person either holds up a warm, fuzzy mirror or a cold, honest one; this becomes the criteria for deciding if a person is "good" or "bad." In other words, if the other person reflects back the blamer is enjoyable or likeable, that person is "good." That's it. If the mirror is good, the person is good. Thus when that person eventually acts rejecting, disagreeable or self-invested, they feel betrayed. They don't get that events and interactions along the way change peoples' perspectives on relationships. It takes work to maintain a relationship. It takes healthy interaction. How we interact over time may drive a person away or draw them closer.

Some families have such a loyalty ethic it doesn't take work. It is required in these families that everyone who belongs is accepted unconditionally. These families are in trouble, however, because a lack of ethics often leads to disaster.

Since blamers or judgers choose whom they will love by the admiring mirror, they don't choose people of quality. How someone makes them feel can be their entire value system and their blinders too. Integrity and self-reflection are not qualities they seek, even though such qualities offer the most safety and the least blame in a relationship. Ultimately, blamers choose people they will later have to blame, if they don't choose people who will later reject them for blaming behavior. For that choice, they hold themselves blameless. A healthy person might ask themselves, "Why didn't I see sooner?" "How did I choose a relationship with a person who doesn't self-reflect?" "How did I come to value this person who now devalues me so for my independent choices?" "How could I be hurt by a mean person's opinion of me?" "What did I do to provoke her?" "Is this about me or him?" Maybe both. A more mature person knows wisdom comes when they own their willingness to sell out integrity for that warm, fuzzy mirror. "When the mirror adored me, I didn't judge the quality of the mirror. Now, that same mirror is my karma for having lacked experience, discretion, discrimination, self-reflection and/or integrity."

A healthy person could not be consistently admiring of anyone, including another healthy person, so ultimately, when the blamer gets a negative mirror, they conclude they were manipulated, misled, conned or tricked, as if once love begins, there is nothing we might do that turns off the spigot. Blamers believe warm mirrors should never change, even when their negative behaviors are introduced into a relationship. They may think the way the other person feels about the blamer should remain steady, or the other person is a fraud. By the same token, loyalty is a critical quality because loyalty means even if the blamer makes mistakes or is retaliatory, there should be no consequences once roles reverse and they become the perpetrator.

Blamers are on a continuum. Some are just pitiful victims of others, while some are killers and rapists. All are blaming others for the horrible way they feel, as if their retaliation will bring them the relief they deserve. Instead of asking for help to stop blaming they defend their right to blame. If we hold killers responsible for an even deeper desire to harm another person, why don't we hold ourselves responsible for retaliation when we're not as badly injured as they once were?

Retaliation as a drive is a disease, if not an epidemic, and it is immature behavior. The epidemic indicates society is far from its capabilities. If we all didn't blame, but opted to understand and adapt, society would be so much healthier.

Blamers are hypocritical thinkers. They cannot handle consequences for their mistakes, but they dish out ruthless consequences for the mistakes others make "against" them, and recruit allies (which typically don't last).

Professional victims cannot seem to own how they have created the disasters in their lives by the relationships they've chosen, the choices they've made and the way they treat people, inflaming decent and even supportive people along the way. Other times they may resentful of people who seem to prefer non-combative, supportive people for company over their explosive manner, as if there was something unjust about how people choose with whom they feel most comfortable. Blamers sometimes think we are all supposed to offer loyalty and the same amount of opportunities or love no matter how they act, even though they, themselves, cannot give such unconditional love.

One of the common complaints blamers make is if someone tries to stop them, especially in the presence of another, they have been harmed for their reputation and actually think if it hadn't been pointed out, no one would have noticed. They may say the observer embarrassed them by telling them they have to stop blaming. They think they should get to blame and maintain their dignity and authority and go unoffended or insulted by corrective feedback, as if they deserve immunity or by having it they would have learned better.

Blamers don't get why some people receive more love and regard than others. I have heard several people accuse PaRC of being a cult because they couldn't achieve acceptance as-is. That loss or failure comes not because of their pathology, but rather because they refused to work on it. They don't get why some people receive more recognition or opportunities than they do. But the good guys, they think, are the ones who give them empathy as they blame for as long as that lasts.

The non-blamers get the most love and regard. They are able to live that way because they had healthy and nurturing childhoods, good role models or coaching or because they did the work to transcend their own drive to blame. Anyone—blamers included—prefers safe and self-reflecting company to judgmental company. Further, those who are more easily despised, such as their enemies and themselves, are damaged from childhood and need to do the work to heal. Blaming gets replaced with insight when one heals.

To get there, one has to choose against blaming and then seriously start reflecting on their drive to blame. They need to decide they are wrong to blame. They have to solicit help to overcome blaming. Overcoming blaming requires a memory of what it felt like to be blamed and how it didn't make us better. It made us worse. It requires a commitment not to turn into the perpetrator. It requires understanding of bad people, who choose not to heal, but a commitment to appreciate those who makes the choice to begin to try to heal. It doesn't mean we have to re-engage. It may mean we have to let it go because we understand their history, our history and our part.

Traits of a Blamer

In blaming or judging, one does enjoy the temporary illusion of superiority, the high of self-righteousness, the transient relief of revenge and the anesthesia of devaluing another. If only we could see ourselves as others see us. Blamers are the lowest on the social ladder. It affords us no status at all, yet some blamers assume a self-righteous pose. Some actually think it will attract empathy and compassion, which it can sometimes do for a short time. Kind people tolerate blamers only for a while out of compassion. Blamers have to do the work to give it up if they want to preserve worthwhile relationships. Otherwise, they are doomed to repeatedly attract and bond with those who also blame, each retaliating in kind, or they lose relationships with non-blamers bitterly and repeatedly.

Blamers have a problem with cause-and-effect thinking. They can't seem to see themselves as others see them or how they created their own dilemma. Usually, they don't realize when they started blaming. This problem impairs their entire quality of life because as long as they see themselves as victims and don't realize they co-create the way people treat them, they limit their opportunities and successes. Yet they failed to properly vet a person or leave a person who was also a blamer. Blamers see cause and effect in terms of how they react when other people treat them badly. Blamers don't see, own, or want to realize what they did to create the reaction against them. All offensive events in their mind begin with the one they perceive as being against them. They seem incapable of looking at what they did, just prior, to inflame the other person. Thus, they are always the victims, even when they are, in fact, the instigators, who just perpetrated an ugly 12 o'clock power play.

Blamers are thin-skinned. Perhaps someone else precipitated the event in question. Maybe it *was* thoughtlessness on the part of the other, maybe even selfishness. Has the blamer never been thoughtless, herself? Perhaps it was a misunderstanding. Perhaps it had nothing to do with them. Perhaps it was a person behaving out of their own pathology and their own childhood, but blamers take these all personally. Then, they move to 12 o'clock because they believe in order to protect themselves, they have to take power over the other by blaming and judging them louder and harder. Conversely, a healthy person would stay calm and humble, at least at first, asking a few clarifying questions and trying to adapt or compromise. An unhealthy person doesn't seek clarification as much as they seek the offense. When blamers assume power to protect themselves, they become the perpetrators. Blamers don't realize *they* are the perpetrators; they became it when they sought to retaliate. They almost always think it's someone else. However, one way to identify the perpetrator is by recognizing who is blaming and assaulting by judging, as well as recognizing who is at 12 o'clock (in power).

While most perpetrators think they are protecting themselves, they are, in fact, unconsciously scapegoating for their past. People who were not so injured in childhood are not so charged. People who are thin-skinned and whose only known defense in life is blaming rather than being blamed will inflame otherwise agreeable people. **Some people are so thin-skinned if a person is not warm and accepting at all times, they experience rejection and become offended.** Empty from childhood and hypervigilant from its traumas and rejections, they anticipate there is another assault coming at any moment. They use arrogance, if not blaming, as a shield. This will always make them wrong because even if they are right in content, they will be wrong in process by blaming or demeaning. In a self-fulfilling prophecy they create the antagonism they anticipate. Then they point to the hostility they created as evidence and justification, unaware their expectations and double standard created the other person's attitude.

Some blamers don't assume power to protect themselves; they assume innocence and seek rescue. As a listener, therapist or mother, I probably can't fix the other party for them, but even if I could, it would be a temporary solution at best. People simply cannot go through life constantly expecting someone else to fix their adversaries for them. It's like giving fish to the poor rather than teaching them how to fish. Blamers need to learn to respond to situations creatively and productively. For example, if they are being stalked, I'm going to ask them how they created it, and how they are trying to get out of it. I will teach them how to extricate themselves from those relationships without inflaming an already pathological personality. I will not join them in discussing what is wrong with the stalker. Insults and name-calling will not help blamers escape their plight; the solution must come from within. It will be in the form of insight into the other.

Sometimes, blamers don't really want to heal or correct anyone; they simply want revenge. Not only that, but they want righteous revenge. Then they don't want to leave the person. They want to stay to destroy them. They want to harm another person, with reassurance from others the person *deserves* it, and to harm them is actually the right thing to do. The trouble with revenge is it leads to more revenge, while self-reflection solves problems and usually allows both or all parties to heal the situation, if not their childhood victimization.

Sometimes people think they are just seeking support when they are blaming. Instead **they are seeking agreement** at the expense of the morals, values and emotional health of their listeners. They use blaming to find comfort, a process that enables and perpetuates blaming. Unhealthy listeners may oblige out of friendship or loyalty because they too think one person alone is to blame. So a "true" friend or "true" therapist may take sides with the blamer or, at least, not judge the blaming. This is dangerous company for a healing person. Each of us is responsible for the quality of the feedback we seek. Loyal or bad feedback entrenches and enables our pathology.

Some blamers think if people are intolerant of blaming, it is because they do not understand the repugnance of the sinner or the horror of the sin. They might think if I am opposed to blaming, I have taken sides with the enemy, given comfort to the culprit, or even blindly idealized the adversary.

Blamers sometimes have a primitive and unconscious fantasy if only the listener, the therapist or the group understood well enough why the blame is on the other party, then they would receive support, and people would take their side. For a therapist, both parties in the couple may try to get the therapist to take their side, so the therapist will "fix the other party." It's a takeoff from the childhood endeavor to get mommy to intervene. If mommy were any good, she would have asked, "What was your part?" When I am working with one member of a couple, I will only address their part. When I work with the other member of the couple, I stay with their part. I will *never* collude with anyone about what is wrong with someone else unless an intervention or break-up is needed.

Blamers often think if they blame hard enough the blamee will get it and become remorseful. This is a popular parenting style too. Blame children or shame them enough and they will change for the better. It's also a popular war philosophy. Blame the other country, insult them, and take them to their knees, and they will learn. But blamees don't become remorseful while they are being blamed. They retaliate the same as the blamer. Blamers and blamees are the same. Neither can stand to be blamed. Both may blame without a clue they each exhibit the characteristics they most despise. They are the enemy and the victim, simultaneously. They are each other.

Blaming is used to make the point "there was nothing I could have done better because what was done to me deprived me of all my choices." **Blaming is one of the traits of a professional victim.** People who have the largest chip on their shoulders and who act the scariest are the biggest victims, even though they think by puffing up, they are refusing to be a victim. Victims retaliate rather than self-reflect, solve problems and grow. Victims find other victims for the 'blaming and retaliation dance.'

Blaming and Complaining to Others

When one is blaming, those who are called upon to listen to the blamer feel like hostages getting burned by a blowtorch. It is not uncommon for blaming and judging to drive healthy people away or to even enrage them. Rather, it is abnormal for a healthy person to not become inflamed at blaming and judging behavior. To tolerate such behavior is to enable it.

Nevertheless, many therapists are trained to remain unmoved by blaming and judging behavior. Actually, I have known therapists to be blamers themselves, so they may collude. On the other hand, many of them build up resentment toward the client because it is an almost inhuman task, and inevitably they know they will be blamed too. Not confronting blaming has its positives and negatives as a treatment style. In my opinion, it is not helpful for the client to miss critical feedback for blaming, even though most therapist fear the wrath of their borderline or narcissistic blaming clients. In this case, the client does not get any reality testing or ethical feedback on how bad blaming and judging is for the sender and the receiver alike. The therapist is just one more person in the client's life to enable the blaming behavior. For sure, this approach is easier than confrontation or teaching responsibility to a blamer who is invested in their victimhood.

If a patient moves into judging and blaming behavior, the traditional therapist does not do the same. She is not committed to correcting the patient's ill-learned childhood lessons, as if it would be too traumatic to be corrected. She has taken the philosophical position that we don't judge or teach morals or values. We allow people to talk and say whatever they want. Eventually, the theory goes, they will figure things out.

It is never too traumatic to be corrected. It is, however, a blow to one's ego, but healing cannot be done with ego. Even though righteous indignation or an expression of repugnance to blaming is a natural consequence, many patients believe they have a right to blame indefinitely. Some therapists are trained blaming is immature at best, destructive at worst. Actually, therapists who also blame are enabled by boards because the training process and boards don't restrict blaming behavior as a sign of immaturity.

Causal therapists, on the other hand, allow themselves to respond fully. They opt for authenticity. They choose natural consequences and do not try to make themselves a blank slate or live underground in the session. They strive to guide by being themselves. They are also able to forgive instantly and move on. They will consistently try to interrupt judging, blaming, "shoulding" or advice giving by whatever means necessary. At PaRC we call it an "arrest." We will interfere so as to stop the patient from blaming another. On occasion, we may let it go to see what happens, but we can't offer and won't offer an accepting face. The sooner the patient relinquishes blaming or judging and moves into expressing their hurt feelings, the sooner their therapist can become empathetic again.

Sometimes **people who blame think they're just getting their feelings out.** Blaming does not get any feelings out at all. Blaming is not a feeling; it's a thought or a judgment. Blaming reinforces bad behavior by practicing it and granting permission to one's self to blame righteously. "That bitch betrayed her marriage vows, and she's a god-damned liar," is a judgment, not a feeling. Expressing this opinion does not reduce the pain, nor does it get feelings out. It has no value. Judging has no value. Blaming has no value. What would have helped them feel better or heal would be to express their pain from having been betrayed and then search their memory for lessons and clues that would have predicted such a betrayal. Then they could make an assessment as to whether or not they would choose to have a future relationship with someone who behaves this way. This is maturity and the goal of mental health.

Blaming begets more blaming. It may feel good or even like a relief, but it actually works itself into a frenzy rather than calms itself down. It heals nothing. Only self-reflection and taking responsibility can heal that which can be healed and redeem whoever can be redeemed. Blamed persons are usually too defensive to self-reflect, and since the blamer is not blameless, the blamed person will become the blamer, and the vicious circle continues.

Intervention

Studies have shown when most people trip, they think, "What is that thing doing in my path?" But if someone else trips, they may think, "They are clumsy" or "They may be on drugs." We tend to think of ourselves as misunderstood but think we perceive other people clearly. We are less at fault, and they are more blameworthy. However, each of us is responsible for everything that happens to us, or at least how we cope with it. Blamers think other people are acting badly, and they are not.

Anyone who tries to seek relief by changing or correcting others will only escalate their own suffering. Unfortunately, blamers may behave this way because they grew up being blamed. This is the rub. To blamers, taking responsibility for their part in an escalating issue would feel like revisiting childhood traumas. Perhaps their parents cruelly blamed them, or maybe they learned to blame in homes where one parent blamed the other, and the child was forced to take sides. Maybe they were never held responsible and are shocked someone would do so. Blamers may have had weak parents who argued with their children. Children become reinforced for arguing and become blamers in the process. In any event, blamers have to transcend this pattern in order to heal. They have to realize everyone is not their father or their mother. They have to realize to join the world of healthy people with all the perks that entails, **they must give up defending and blaming and self-reflect instead**.

In order to give up blaming, we have to choose to take 100% responsibility for everything happens to us. If we do, then we see our mistakes faster, and we self-correct faster. We finally become mature. That's what mature people know and understand. In taking responsibility for our actions we discover self-awareness and personal responsibility. So, if someone abused us, we were supposed to leave and end it. If we don't leave a blamer, we are responsible for staying because there are hurtful people in this world, and the only way to deal with them is to not indulge them and let them get away with bad behavior. If we leave blamers, they may finally learn to stop blaming. If they give up blaming, they may attract healthy people who treat them right. Blamers don't get to attract healthy people. A blamer would say the other should stay and take it. But, that is immature thinking that actually keeps us down, so we are unsuccessful and unlovable. The more we take 100% responsibility for the results of our actions, the sooner we realize we create the way the other person treats us by how we treat them.

I tolerate no blaming in either party, and instead, may wistfully await the natural consequences each person elicits. I know each party will reap their own karma, if they continue to act out. I forever hope blamers will finally stop and self-reflect, ending the resistance. Sometimes I erupt out of intolerance to blaming, especially if the client presumes to instruct me, and especially if they are going back on their agreement to let me teach. This is a healthy and normal visceral response to blaming, even though blamers may loathe or think is beneath a therapist, or even unhealthy. What a blamer seeks is a comforting response for blaming, as if comfort is evidence they are understood and righteous. I want blamers to know **comfort will come if they stay in their hurt feelings**, not in their mental judgments.

Often I try to show blamers their part, to get them to start self-reflecting and stop blaming, and sometimes they decide I am not safe. Sometimes when blamers hear my feedback, they explode, thinking they are being blamed rather than handed an opportunity for personal insight. I have encountered students who seem to enter what appears to be the ultimate, intolerable mind warp, as I ask them to self-reflect on their own actions and whether they seem to play a role in creating such events. The mind warp seems to be they are being treated like the assaulter, when, in their mind, they are clearly the assaulted, only retaliating. The blamer may experience feedback as a betrayal, if the blamer doesn't understand. Yet everyone has their part and all anyone can do constructively in a situation is to look at their own part. When they don't want to look at their part, they are stuck, blind and have become the offender. They and their offender are now the same.

Some think an objection to blaming is blaming itself. This is a kind of double-think. Plainly said, it is not blaming to criticize blaming; it is mirroring. Sometimes defensive blamers think their listeners have one standard for their enemy and another for them because, certainly, if their listeners could see the bad guy clearly, they would take their side against him. Maybe, they think, any objection to blaming tolerates the behavior of the enemy. This is just a lack of insight into the dynamic of blaming behavior.

It is our video game of perils and traps. We were born into this game, and it is our job to navigate the landscape without blaming the landscape. Ultimately, we can navigate out of the most dangerous pitfalls into the ones that induce growth if we make good choices. If we stop and make friends with a dragon because that dragon is worth a lot of points, then we are responsible for choosing that relationship. We are responsible for assessing those with whom we choose to partner up, and further, we are responsible for our part in how that relationship goes. We are never justified in behaving badly, not even when the other party did it first. If we see someone with whom we chose to partner acting unethically toward someone else, know the day will come when they are unethical with you.

Richard Ramirez told me in an interview once, speaking about himself in the third person, The Night Stalker once came upon a woman who was seated in her den. She looked up and saw him. She said, "Oh my God. Who did this to you?" He sat down and spoke with her for 20 minutes and then got up and left her there, safe. I am saying **there is almost no person who is so villainous if you have an opportunity to treat them well that they won't give you their best.** If there are exceptions to this rule, then there is still no virtue in living our lives in anticipation of those exceptions. As soon as we begin to treat someone badly, the odds are set they will give us their worst. Knowing that, if we still treat them badly, we are looking for the fight we get.

If you are in a divorce, don't play dirty because she started to play dirty. Try to turn it around. Try lion taming, as I think of it, like the woman who tamed The Night Stalker. At best, I can advise you to **see what you can do in the future to head off such situations by helping you see how you participated in creating this one**. The deepest healing and growth can only come from a quiet, defenseless self-reflection in which you take the time to visualize how you acted and what you provoked in the other person that would have been intolerable to them, just as it would have been to you. It is fruitless to focus on what the other person should have been like. The goal of mental health is to be able to navigate through all circumstances with all types of people in a healthy way, possibly steering your course to a healthier terrain, but it is never to change all the people with whom you interact, so they will treat you better, certainly not by blame, force, or threat.

Blamers often think there should be unconditional marriages and even friendships. They should get to act however they want to act. They will seek evidence you are wrong for criticizing their blaming, and, as a matter of fact, you are the one to blame. At the point you **ask for evidence of your wrong actions**, they will get very vague but protest that you found any fault with them. They are so fragile inside and so mean outside.

Blamers sometimes argue if they give up blaming, they would have to walk around unconditionally accepting all the bad behavior in the world. They think they will be unable to defend themselves and they won't get to offer their disdain for wrong actions. Yet, they are responsible for their choices. If they choose only healthy people with whom to relate, that is, people who self-reflect on their mistakes, they will not need to blame anyone. The hitch is healthy people won't want to associate with blamers, only with people who also self-reflect.

If you have made your way to PaRC, and you are asserting we are not good enough here, then I suppose to you you have been confronted for blaming, but I submit you are running out of land and people, if this community is not good enough. I have been around, and I find those who are working on themselves here are truly dedicated. I rather dare you to find a better place to interact and get guidance. If you do, let me know because I have always wanted to be able to offer people choices, not just PaRC. Here you will find people who have signed on to use healthy interaction skills and to stand corrected when they don't. I don't know of a safer place. Here, you take responsibility for your choices, your skills, and if you find yourself in a relationship with someone who does not take responsibility for her choices and her skills, then you ask them to get on board more than once. If they decline, you need to move on. Moving on is part of taking responsibility for your choices.

Maturity

If the demand to regard our mate or friend is unreasonable, we must leave. Kicking them out is inflammatory. If we don't like it, we leave. If we leave with grace absent blaming, we may be offered the house. If we stay, we are choosing to be a victim so we can hold the title of the innocent one and can then righteously blame. We are driven to find fault with anyone who hurt us, even if the person is remorseful and no longer offending. we believe as long as we suffer from the assault we report, we are entitled to blame. We then hold on to that injury so we can maintain the righteous upper hand. The trouble with that is blaming the person who injured us, while they are not fighting back, makes us the perpetrator. We have imprinted their behavior. We give back what we got. Now we escalate. Now we are them. They are us.

Blaming is a dance. It is a dance that began before we met. It has a history and may go back for generations past and last generations to come. Treating someone with faith like The Night Stalker was treated once can save you suffering. Blaming or projecting onto someone what they will do can be dangerous. Truman Capote tells the story of two escaped prisoners who made a B-line to the farm house of a successful family business where there was said to be a safe with lots of money. They got there and the safe only held personal papers. They were sorely disappointed and had to buy time to think. They tied up the mother, father, teen son and teen daughter, but took good care of them, brought meals on trays, provided a pitcher of water, aspirin at their bedside, tissues and other supplies found at the crime scene. After they murdered the entire family and were arrested, Capote went to their jail to interview the more intelligent one of the two. He said he couldn't talk because he was on trial for his life. Capote made him a deal he couldn't refuse, offering to pay for the best attorney available, if after the trial, whatever the verdict, an interview would be provided. So after the two were sentenced to death, and Capote's reputation had been tarnished for providing their attorney, Capote came back for his interview. He spoke to Perry Edward Smith, asking the question of all questions: "If you knew you were going to kill all of them, why did you take such good care of them until the end?" "We didn't plan to kill them," Smith said. "The old man kept saying, 'I know you're going to kill us,' so I got tired of hearing it and I took a knife and cut his throat. After that, we had to kill the rest of them."

I have told you about the power of projections in self-fulfilling prophesy. I have shown you how compassion spared a life and expectations killed. No one demonizes another for having been misunderstood or disrespected, if they are mature and healthy. It is those of us who have injuries inside of worthlessness that take the bait. We think we are in search of the perfect person who will never hurt us, and if those we engage do hurt us, we get to defend ourselves by being tough, blaming and rejecting. We further prove one can trust no one.

Blaming is immature. Projecting worst outcomes creates them. Mature people take responsibility for the problem, find their part, try to understand the experience of the other and then respectfully seek to negotiate a solution that is ethical and/or acceptable to both parties. How bad we were originally injured is never an excuse to retaliate, except in the moment.

When one has lived a lifetime thinking "either/or" thoughts, it is not possible to simply introduce a new blameless way of thinking, especially one that can be digested with a simple reading. There have been times when I have tried to bust this blame-based thinking, and my student has interpreted my intervention as an attempt to deprive them of all their rights to feelings, to reason on their own behalf and to protect themselves. Some say they have a right to hold a grudge and keep blaming until they don't have the pain anymore. Some might think surely I simply do not understand them, their circumstances, or how bad or unusual is their problem. They think I don't get they have been dealt an unfair blow to the solar plexus not unlike betrayal, so I can't understand their plight. If I did, I would not seek to deprive them of their right to blame.

If we had those mature and healthy traits we would think differently. We would think we chose a damaged person. What were we thinking? How did we miss the clues? Then we were unhealthy in the way we dealt with them, so we inflamed the situation. They won't change by blaming. We make them worse by blaming. We could get ourselves killed by blaming. If they did change, it would come from regard, safe self-reflection, understanding, therapy and, I dare say, knowledge of new relationship skills.

Maybe we have picked badly, and they are as bad as we say, but we chose them, and we need to un-choose them after having spoken kindly on how we feel being targeted and disrespected. Then we leave with appreciation for all the things we shared without further blame. There is no more dangerous time in our lives than when we both blame and coldly, arrogantly leave, or worse.

We are all born immature. Our job is to mature. This is true for individuals, nations and evolution. Immature people blame, judge and seek retaliation. They see others as separate from them and do not recognize their part in the interaction. They do not yet get everyone else's needs to be treated with regard as much as we need to be treated with regard. Kick them out. Retaliation drives to destroy reach their highest level when we reject someone this way. We could get killed.

The Autopsy

Now the autopsy can begin. As a student, we can look back over the ways we were treated as children and how the perhaps cruel, contentious, dysfunctional or neglectful ways of our parents have become our own imprinted coping mechanisms, including the promise to ourselves we won't let anyone ever hurt us again. We can remember how we were treated and how we incorporated the blame game into our defense mechanisms. We can see how our parents learned from their parents and how there is a chain reaction from generation to generation. No one was born bad. No one was born enlightened. No one was born evil. **No one knew any better than what they learned at home.** If you believe you are as you are because you were genetically engineered, you may miss the opportunity to self-correct. Even the most genetically oriented research now admits or suggests there are no genetically driven behaviors without being first triggered by environment. You can change if you choose to change and agree to be taught as a humble student.

As students we can look at the adult years that all our inflammatory actions provoked further tragedy. We can see how we failed to choose a healthy person with whom to have a relationship because we ourselves were unhealthy. We haven't earned or attracted safe people ourselves. We can see holding onto grudges or morbid expectations heals no one, and in fact, recreates the cycle of revenge. We can see holding onto grudges proves we too are prone to the retaliation behavior that originally hurt us. We became the perpetrator as we became the victim.

At one time I thought, "If I take responsibility for my choices, I will be blamed." I have also thought, "If I cop to this, I will look bad, and they will use it against me." Yet, responsibility is not about blame. Blaming—vs. responsibility—has an unforgiving property. It projects there is no hope in the blamer. There is also no hope for the blamed. It means the blamed is irredeemable, unforgiven, forever deserving of mistrust or deserving of punishment, if not shunning. They are the way they are and will not change. The drive to judge or blame is a drive to scar, to retaliate, even to destroy the blamed person, if not to set them back so far that self-reflection would be a waste of their time. When one blames, both parties get worse. When one blames, one is self-indulgent without consideration of how we create one another, whether or not the blaming makes the other person a better person or a worse person. If we blame to indulge ourselves without any intention to build the other person, we are perpetrators now. We have been wronged, but now we have become the entitled blamer.

I have often recommended someone leave a person they blame and cannot seem to forgive. When I make this suggestion, the person often experiences a moment of speechlessness that I get how bad the other person is, siding with them that they should leave. It is usually followed by a recommitment to martyrdom by staying. Then I say, "No, this is for their sake, not yours. They cannot heal while you blame."

There are people who teach those who have committed domestic violence and betrayals of infidelity by telling them they will have to tolerate questioning until they have proven they are trustworthy. This is not to be a blank check for the victim, however, wherein the victim can seek endless revenge. That only creates two perpetrators, given you consider emotional abuse hurtful, as I do. It's actually another variation on domestic violence.

Some people take a position they will not give respect until they get it. That is a lost cause. It is delusional. It is unenlightened and immature. It is blind and ignorant. We don't give love, respect and understanding to people who demand it. These people often insist, by virtue of the content of the issue, they are correct that they have been wronged. Finally such a position, which may be right in content, is wrong in process. A demand for unearned respect in the name of our victimhood will drive people away. If we are afraid giving up blaming would make people take us for granted and disrespect us, then we do not understand people respect most the people who don't blame. They stay where there is no blame, but there is respect. We give respect to get respect.

Changing

We can make a choice to give up blaming. If we make the choice, we can have loving guidance through the eye of the needle with our therapist. Students safely ponder other ways they could have handled things. We can see how people responded to our blaming and then we can remember when we were in a similar situation, responding likewise to feeling blamed. With each memory we can see alternative ways we could have coped; thus we begin the process of rewiring. Seeing begets change. Seeing, finally, is change. If someone whom we blame allows us to continue blaming them after apologizing and attempting to self-reflect, we are bad for them and must be advised they should leave. One would need to see the therapist or friend or spiritual advisor did the right thing in recommending this to them. They should leave us because we blame them too much. If we can't see that, we are in deep.

How much we want to heal is what will make us well. Not revenge. Our target was once in our shoes, having been the victim and then choosing to perpetrate us. It's a chain reaction. That's why The Golden Rule is born of insight; if we don't turn the other cheek, we pass it on.

For this reason, I suggest whoever embraces this contract would do well to read it and re-read it repeatedly. I believe each reading will help to unravel a little more. A blamer will ultimately enter into a state of confusion before fortunately landing on the other side of wisdom. If they keep reading, there will be a profound realization. I guarantee it. If one can stay humble and endure this disorientation long enough, reading as often as possible, qualitative change may follow. It will be as if the mind turned over. Previous categories will begin to dissolve, while others make enough sense to take over. Sometimes this happens in one moment. Sometimes it is slow and certain. Either way, the pay-off is there for those who pursue. The personality will make a profound shift leading to a rebirth of sorts, a la William James (*Varieties of Religious Experience*).

An RSW is a good environment for wiring in new experiences and new skills, but the theory needs to be embraced for the turnover to take place. If you choose to work on blaming, please do not simply read and sign the No Blame Contract. Sign it, commit to it, and then take the hours, days, weeks and perhaps months studying it until you make it your own. To do so may mark the end of a personality disorder, defined very much by the drive to blame or to reign. Finally, leave your ego under your pillow. Be willing to be a "nobody" or a "nothing" for at least six months. Stop defending yourself as much as possible. The truth is there is nothing to defend. At your core, you are divine. Now that you are an adult, only your beliefs, projections and coping skills can cause you trouble, and they can be replaced with skills that create positive results if you let yourself unlearn and relearn.

Stop representing how hurt you are. Hurt is something that needs to be briefly expressed to others but processed alone or with a therapist. If you are loitering and perseverating, you are reinjuring yourself. You are not processing your part in the situation.

In order to make the change from blamer to a mature, personally responsible party, one must be humble and in a state of surrender. You have to think of yourself as a hero, your own hero, instead of a victim. In this state, one self-reflects. In this state, one owns their own truths and their own motives. In this state, one can see the drive to avenge one's own childhood pain upon another while refusing to understand and forgive someone who is remorseful for having injured us. When we are humble, we can cry for our own wounds, especially for our childhood wounds, so we can heal and move on. Simply put, in order to heal from this blaming disorder, one will have to choose to give up power for a while and own the wounds we don't want to own from our parents. That doesn't mean we are to disrespect our parents. It means we learn to cry for ourselves, so we don't scapegoat and hurt others.

To learn not to blame requires a careful consideration of our relationships, including how we choose people and how we want to change people to meet our needs, rather than give them understanding so they will appreciate us in return. We will need to consider how we have come to project onto them our mistrust and contempt, and how that inflames them. We will need to see how the relationship evolved based upon real time interactions and could not live on promises alone.

We cannot afford to have any relationships with others who are blamers too, unless they too are doing the work to change. Some have elected to relate to no one else for six months other than their co-workers, therapist and their RSW. In order to turn this blaming thing around we must surrender to a humble state, giving up claims to power and pride, giving up revenge, giving up 12 o'clock, as I call it, and seeking the egoless state of 6 o'clock, which includes faith and surrender, thus inviting transformation.

Zen Buddhism is the only religion without beliefs. It is essentially ethicism. It guides us into clear seeing by identifying our false beliefs about ourselves, others and the world in order to see clearly. It helps make healthy, mature choices. For this reason I use Zen as a template for healing that includes universal religious wisdom. When we see clearly, we increase our self-worth and the regard of others. Here are some simple steps:

- Realize there is nothing wrong with you. You were born divine and are as divine as you allow yourself to be.
- There is nothing to defend, other than your behavioral choices, but plenty to understand.
- Wake up. Pay attention to others, the situation and yourself. Stop reacting. See.
- Sit quietly to observe your thoughts and identify wrong thoughts.
- Assume there is always suffering in life; trying to live to avoid suffering is foolish.
- Avoiding and judging our own pain is hopeless and useless. Instead, visit the pain courageously and calmly to see what message it brings. Focus on the pain and "listen."
- Identify the lies you have come to believe and promote in your own head: some to defend yourself, some to injure yourself on behalf of someone else (your parent, parents, bullies), and some to promote blame and adversity.
- Take 100% responsibility for your life. Try not to play the victim.
- Become a lion tamer and bring out the good in others by respecting them, even when they don't deserve it. Do the right thing when it is in front of you to do, even if you don't feel like it. This is how you get respect. This is how you earn your feelings of self-worth. This is how you fill the aching hole inside of you.

The Dignity of Coping

Where there is no blaming, but maybe the honest expression of vulnerable feelings and preferred ethics, we become a magnet. Others want to offer us respect and start returning regard. We discover respect is earned, and we are not entitled to unearned respect. It is this type of person who attracts regard, love and understanding. This type of person is not living in the Dark Ages. This type of person is mature and enlightened.

When people take responsibility for choices that backfire, they have dignity, honor and health. Taking responsibility for one's choices and consequences empowers one to grow. Almost all successful and great people take responsibility for their choices, even when the other party assaulted them. Listening to one take responsibility is uplifting and engenders great regard vs shame.

I love Zen stories because they are so helpful. There is the story of the young maiden whose father was a highly regarded businessman in her village, and it was the same village in which a Zen master drew followers from throughout the land. One day she admitted she was with child, and her father demanded to know what man she had lain with. He pushed and pushed her to reveal her secret. She knew her father was in a blaming mood, so she would not speak. Finally, she had to give him a name, so she said it was the venerable Zen Master. When the baby was born, the businessman took the child to the Zen Master and handed the baby boy over, saying, "You have destroyed my reputation. You should be ashamed of yourself." The Zen master did not defend himself. He simply said, "Is that so?" taking the tiny child. One day the daughter could stand it no longer and went to her father to say, "I lied. The father of my baby is the handsome fisherman by the wharf." The businessman went to the Zen Master and apologized profusely saying, "I am so terribly sorry. I have ruined your reputation," to which the master said, "Is that so?" as he returned the wee one to his grandfather. The most powerful line in the story is when the daughter "could stand it no longer." Stand what no longer? When we blame someone, and they don't defend themselves, the blamer is stuck. Their subconscious mind needs reaction to justify their blaming. If we don't react, that is the most powerful thing we can do. Anyone looking on will decide we are cool, and our blamer is off-the-wall wrong about us. Not fighting back is incredibly powerful. It awakens a sleeping conscience.

In another story, a Zen master sits in his hut when he is surprised by the entry of a thief who demands he turn over his most valuable possession, his robe. The Zen master takes off his garb and hands it to him, saying, "You will need food too," as he provides a dish of food in his favorite bowl. "Oh," he added, "You need to thank me," and so the thief thanked him and sheepishly left with his food and robe. Shortly thereafter, the thief was brought to the hut by the local authorities with his wrists tied, as the officer recognized the master's robe. The master said, "Oh, no, I gave it to him. He was very cordial, and he thanked me." The thief became his student in that moment and became a Zen master himself in later years.

My Zen master told a story from his life. He said he fell in love with and married a woman who loved Zen Buddhism as much as he did. They made a beautiful baby girl together, but one day, a dude showed up at the Zen center, and she was enamored. The two of them took off across the country on his Harley and returned two weeks later. My Zen master was left with his baby girl. He was enraged and spoke of how he was going to get custody of the child and his soon-to-be-ex-wife would never see the little girl again. Shortly thereafter, there was a Zen retreat of sorts called a Sesshin. In a Sesshin meditation starts at 6 am and ends at 9 pm, with some ritualistic meals, a little walking in circles and chanting to get the circulation going again. There is no talking and the retreat goes on for days with a ceremony and sermon at the end to break the silence. Well, my soon-to-be-sensei was a student with his own master, and he was given a special place to sit and meditate facing his wife and her new sweetie. For days they faced one another and at the end of the retreat, he spoke to her and said, "You may take our daughter with my hopes you will let me see her. You are her mother," to which she said, "Please keep her and allow me to visit whenever I am ready or able." He agreed. Bullying is no way to lead. My Zen master modeled maturity.

I have nearly always found if I became humble when I was wrong; if I sought to solve problems when I erred; if I simply said, "Oops," I was safe and respected. In very few cases have I encountered someone who wanted to target me when I was humble and owning my mistake, gaining some satisfaction from rubbing it in or enjoying the opportunity for dominance. I have always used that as a most successful tool to detect those with whom I would not be safe in a relationship. If I make a mistake and self-reflect, how do they act? That's key. If they blame, I need to tell them at least three times if they continue to blame after I have self-reflected, I will have to depart the relationship. Less than three times is bad skills. A person deserves feedback and a warning before we leave them. Three times gives them a minimum of two opportunities to begin the work to change before I leave. In cases of true domestic violence, there is no need to warn. Just leave.

When working to heal in therapy there is a period where the patient is empowered by their therapist to "blame" their parents (in empty chair work, unsent letters, dialogue). I believe it is the essential time in one's adult life where blaming is appropriate because it leads to purging childhood injuries, without which the adult child will scapegoat others. The truth is, it's not really blaming. It's processing what never got processed. A healthy process includes, "When you… I felt" or "When you… I feel." There are many variations on I-messages, as opposed to You-messages. Whenever we want to express ourselves and we start out with "You," we are about to make the other person feel blamed. We must stick to "I" and represent our feelings, which gives the listener room to regret with empathy.

If we are victims of anyone else after childhood, especially as adults, we need to find our part. Even if we were raped or the victim of a drunk driver, our part includes how much we buy into the experience as defining. We already know there are rapists out there and people who drive drunk. The world is filled with danger. It's our video game. How we cope will determine our resilience.

If we can't find our part, we are in more trouble than our victimhood. There are traumatic events adults endure and can require some raging and crying and purging feelings of profound hurt. That should be done in the therapy office or with a loving family member. But it is a temporary process that should yield insights that enable one to walk away from the victimhood. If one gets stuck, they preserve their role as the blamer or the perpetrator. Mature people move on. I have seen mothers and fathers of murdered victims ask the judge not to execute their child's murderer. These people are evolved and mature. That doesn't mean they didn't rage and grieve. It just means they understand perpetrating begets perpetrating, which is The Golden Rule of "Do unto others as we would have them do unto us."

Finding Good Enough People

How loveable one is results from the qualities they cultivate in themselves. Blamers think love is unfairly distributed, which is true for infants and children. A person who takes pride in how scary he is when he's threatened should not be surprised healthy people want to steer clear of him. If he put that much energy into taking responsibility for all his experiences, especially his mistakes, others would prefer him. Healthy and safe people love those who would rather grow than take revenge. Healthy people may offer compassion, and they are often kind enough to support a blamer in pain for a while, hoping the blamer will pull out of it. However, no healthy person will stay indefinitely in a relationship with a deviant blamer.

Healthy people frequently give feedback, usually honest feedback. They may say, "As long as you drink, I can't stay in your life and watch you self-destruct," or "When you insult me so, I feel hurt and I want to get away from you." "When you speak with so much judgment, I want to avoid you." "When you demean me or boss me around, I want to leave you." "When I am the only one self-reflecting, I want to give up on the relationship." A healthy person will let you know how they feel when your actions and words are thoughtless or designed to be hurtful. They will tell you if they dislike your moral choices, arrogance or judgmental behavior. They will set boundaries for themselves and maintain them, even if it hurts your feelings. Healthy people will themselves accept valid mirrors and criticism to grow on, and they will make choices that are correct, even when it really hurts to do the right thing.

Once a healthy person sees they are in a relationship with a blaming and non-self-reflecting person, they will have no regrets leaving, while ironically, a blaming person will lament the loss of a person who fails to self-correct. As a matter of fact, many if not most therapists acknowledge they have to refer judgmental narcissist and blaming borderline patients to other therapists who can handle their judging and blaming. They are considered the most difficult clients with whom to work. They are the most draining for a therapist. Many if not most therapists choose not to work with borderline or narcissistic patients.

Blamers and judgers may hate people who give them a true mirror of how they seem to others. They may hate people who offer them this gift of truth at great expense to the relationship. They may consider the person who is investing in them enough to bravely offer honest feedback as rude, cruel or elitist. They may blame the healthy person.

Unfortunately blamers would rather stay ignorant of how they are perceived and what people are thinking about them. Yet to know how we are perceived and what people think about us is the greatest opportunity we could have to self-correct. Without that information, we can never improve our social relatedness. But blamers pretend if they don't know what people are thinking about them, then people aren't thinking anything bad about them. They may even think they can argue someone out of their observations and thoughts. What would change the healthy person's thoughts, however, would be a change and apology. In order to grow, we have to come to love the mirror, no matter how painful it is for our egos. Actually, the mirror is easiest on us when we give up our egos and giving up our egos is easiest when we finally realize we are not our behavior. Behaviors are simply the coping mechanisms we learned in childhood, and at the time, they were brilliant adaptations. Now those coping mechanisms are obsolete. Behavior can be easily changed and none of it is who we really are anyway. Once we accept the challenge, surrender, and relinquish blaming, we are no longer blamers.

Your No-Blame Contract with Yourself

I agree to be responsible for my own actions and choices. I understand by so doing, I will sometimes have to make choices that go against my feelings. I understand making choices that are difficult in the short run will enhance the quality of my life in the long run. I intend to recognize the red flags that inform me I am in a situation I need to leave or clarify. I intend to recognize the ramifications of my choices.

If someone chooses not to be in a relationship with me, I shall accept that choice with grace. I understand how much I deserve relationships with good people has to do with how I behave in life. If people don't like me, that is their choice and my consequence. I have to make myself a person with whom people want to spend time. I don't get to be cherished or in relationships just because I want it. When I make mistakes, I don't get to claim ignorance. It is my job to see and learn what I did to cause their reaction to me. It is also my responsibility to assess and choose well who I bring into my life.

I understand I am responsible for the quality of my close relationships, friendships, partnerships and romantic choices. I will ask my friends and loved ones to be ethical toward others and me, as I will be ethical toward others and them. If I know someone who is willing to betray another, cheat another, or to keep a secret that needs to be aired, I will ask that friend to correct his or her actions. If the corrections are not made, I understand I am putting myself at risk by staying in the relationship. I am responsible for remaining in an ongoing dysfunctional relationship where the warnings were clear and easy to read. If I fail to heed the warnings that come to me, I am the fool, no matter how passionate and loving my intentions. Further, I don't get to blame the person with whom I chose to stay in a relationship, since their actions were a pattern known to me from the beginning, if not now. With whom I choose to relate is always my responsibility. If I seek relationships from the large population of unreliable people, that is my doing. If I exit a relationship in such a way as to leave a person feeling more rejected, more injured, or more insulted than need be, then I am responsible for extra consequences at the end of that relationship.

I understand if I am in a relationship, wherein for some significant reason I cannot leave, I am responsible for my part in making that relationship work. At no time, no matter how badly they treat me, am I entitled in this theory to resort to arrogance, blaming or judging. I may assess the parties involved in order to figure out the most calming way to communicate with them. I commit to treat all people with respect, to seek clarity and understanding, and to not take their bad behavior personally, except for the behavior I provoked. On the other hand, I accept there is a multitude of people in this world trying to get even for their childhood and how badly they treat me is not necessarily about me. I simply need to vet and avoid relationships with these people, unless they are working on themselves. How I respond is about me. I do not intend to escalate any bad situations, but I intend to learn ways to de-escalate all situations. I do not deserve relationships with healthy, thoughtful, self-reflecting people if I am not able to act as maturely as they do. I will always assume there is something I am doing to inflame any situation. Thus I will always be seeking to self-reflect and self-correct in difficult situations from which there seems no escape.

I will do the right thing when it is in front of me to do, no matter how difficult. I will make the right choices and speak consciously with relationship skills. I will do my part to seek clarity, understanding and conciliation. I will avoid retribution, blame and judgment.

If I have elected to have a child, I commit to being a True Parent. That is, I will stay home with the child or ensure the child's other parent stays home for the first five years of life. I will sell what I need to in order to stay home. I will reduce my lifestyle to near poverty if necessary, to ensure my child enjoys a secure attachment in the first five years of life. I will not fight over the custody of my child unless it is to ensure a continuous attachment. I will not seek to change the primary caregiver of my child unless the primary caregiver has already harmed my child's ability to attach. If I have failed my child, I will take responsibility for how he or she is turning out and make the necessary corrections as soon as possible.

I am not promising to be perfect, nor do I expect others to be perfect. I am committing to self- reflect as soon as I am able when things are going badly. I am agreeing if I begin to judge or blame, my therapist is expected to try to stop me. I am making it my goal to accept others as they are, to accept my own imperfections, while learning to self-correct in order to make my life more rewarding.

I will take responsibility for the quality of my life. Thus when I make bad choices, I accept the results gracefully. I shall work to correct my mistakes and to make amends where appropriate. I don't blame others because I have in my power the ability to assess those with whom I choose to relate. I—and I alone—am responsible for the quality of my life.

By signing the Signature Page, I invite and agree to corrective feedback. If I fall into a moment of retaliation without self-reflection, I can expect to be reminded I signed this contract and agreed to do this work. Therefore if I suffer an "arrest," I acknowledge it is in my agreement, and I am prepared today to accept the consequences of my actions as much as I may loathe them. Anyone with whom I work on this commitment to grow and self-correct has my permission to hold me accountable for breaking the agreement, even if it is inconvenient or embarrassing. I am assured I can get back on track with the simplest acknowledgement because there is no one as lovely as someone who gets humble and self-corrects. In that moment I may have found my highest, most holy self.

Causal Theory Practices

You understand you are being encouraged to make it your therapeutic and lifestyle goal to live an open lifestyle free of secrecy and adversarial relationships in your private life. You commit to telling your therapist issues you have with this recommendation so s/he may be apprised of special circumstances that may be honored, and s/he may begin helping you work these issues through, so you will no longer be saddled with unnecessary and harmful secrets. You acknowledge you've read the Causal Theory Practices below by signing the separate Signature Page.

I. CAUSAL THERAPY IS LIKE ZEN TRAINING. Causal Therapy involves a rigorous approach to healing, which is quicker and deeper, but it involves greater commitment, openness, courage and humbleness. You have been told this type of training is for a particular type of student who wants to accelerate and deepen their work. This process may include direct feedback and instruction.

II. HUMILITY and SURRENDER. You understand the primary qualities required to heal—and especially to do this work—are humility and surrender, the ability to drop one's ego or pride in order to address blind spots. Humility is the quality that makes a student teachable. If this is a problem for you but you are willing to submit to the process anyway, you could be surprised by your ability to grow. If you cannot submit, this is not the therapy style for you.

III. CAUSAL UNDERSTANDING OF CONFIDENTIALITY AND SECRECY. You have read the essay on Confidentiality and Secrecy included in this packet.

IV. CONTINUING STUDY. You have been advised for optimal results you need to study the Causal Theory at least four times. You may do so by doing any combination of the following: attending the live Parenting Series, listening to the condensed CDs (4 hrs), listening to the complete CDs (16 hrs), watching the complete DVDs (16 hrs), and/or reading *The Manual*.

V. NO BLAMING OR JUDGING. You agree to be taught not to blame in the Relationship Skills Workshop as well as in your life. You have read and will continue to study the No Blame Contract.

VI. INTAKE. You are expected to complete the Intake Questionnaire before beginning therapy.

VII. NO HIDDEN DYNAMICS. You understand as a member of a Relationship Skills Workshop, you are responsible for acting with integrity with all members of the RSW. You will not unnecessarily or unreasonably keep secrets from the group regarding relevant aspects of your process. Nor will you ask another member to keep a secret from the group. Any dialogue relevant to the work in the RSW belongs to the group, including telecommunications with other members of the group, your therapist or coach. In other words, members of the group may share emails, texts and voicemail messages from you relating to issues at hand, so the group may ascertain your use of relationship skills for proper mirroring of my process.

VIII. PRIVACY AND CONFIDENTIALITY. You will not divulge the names of any persons in your RSW along with any information about them to anyone outside the workshop, including persons who once belonged to the workshop, but have terminated. You may discuss lessons learned in the workshop process without naming names.

IX. CONSEQUENCES. You acknowledge you have been forewarned if you misuse this process and bring harm to the reputation of anyone in your RSW by using content disclosed or discussed against them and/or by reporting information about them to someone outside the process. While this rule intends to protect everyone in workshop or RSW, it is especially critical for members who have high-profile professions. If any information learned in this process is used against anyone you may be terminated from PaRC permanently.

X. MODELING OPENNESS. You have been informed you will meet people in PaRC who have elected to live an open lifestyle, who do not object to being discussed in and out of workshop or RSW as long as what is said is truthful and constructive. You may look at them as models of mental health.

XI. NO TERMINATING IN THE MIDDLE OF AN ISSUE. If you terminate in the middle of an issue, by disappearing or by telecommunication, that information may be shared with the RSW as well. Members of the RSW will be allowed to discuss and evaluate your termination process in order to seek closure.

XII. FOREWARNING OF A CRITICAL ISSUE. Before your therapy is concluded, you will probably be challenged with an issue by your therapist if not someone else, if it is not yet apparent you can process an issue with skill—with humbleness, openness and clarifying questions. You may even be misunderstood. This may be the only sure way to ascertain your relationship skills. You will not blame the other party for misunderstanding you; instead you will accept life is, in part, a series of misunderstandings and attempt to problem-solve.

XIII. RIGHT TO WITHHOLD TREATMENT. Your therapist reserves the right to withhold treatment and refer you to another type of therapy or therapist upon request if you do not agree to the above items.

XIV. CONSULTATION. You are hereby advised your therapist may be discussing your case in Consultation, where interns, trainees, coaches and other therapists consult regarding PaRC cases.

Relationship Skills

The Premise

All of us were born good and innocent. We uniquely learned how to adapt to our environments. Now those adaptations no longer serve us. We will be unlearning and relearning healthy interaction skills here. We will be receiving feedback on our beliefs about ourselves and others and how we are representing ourselves so we may change as quickly as we are willing. Everyone will be protected from old mirrors, shoulding, judging, advice giving (unless asked), or blaming. Anyone who treats another as if they are inherently bad will be placed under arrest. In other words, there are moments in RSW in which a member may be disciplined or stopped from treating another in a harmful way. All members are entitled to such safety. The values of The Theory are paramount, and no one will be the exception. When someone is under arrest, it is temporary and lasts only as long as they are a threat to someone else.

Skills Guidelines

Beginning

- New people: get the lay of the land before jumping in (the best way to be a new person on the block).
- Leave your ego at the door. Practice being at six o'clock. Don't spread your arms wide or put your hands in a tent unless you choose to look arrogant.
- Be prepared to speak in unfamiliar and "unnatural" words until you can say them in your own words.
- Be prepared to learn the hard way: Baptism by fire.
- Begin all relationships in faith, never suspicion. End them for an ongoing refusal to self-reflect or for a mutually agreed upon incompatibility (after thorough discussion).
- Do not dominate the air space or talk down to people.
- Don't waste precious time thinking about what you should say to look good.

Resolving Issues

- Stage One is an issue from outside the forum. Stage Two is a live issue in the room. Stage Twos take precedence over everything else. Never let a Stage Two wait, inside or outside RSW.
- There are two skills of disagreement: The Change Model ("When you …"), and Mirroring. The former is subjective and said at six o'clock in feelings. The latter is objective and said impartially. Neither is offered at twelve o'clock.
- Use the template: "Ouch!" "I feel…when you…" "When you… I see…" "When you…I have the thought that…"
- Never presume to know a person's motives, but you can check an impression of motives by asking with spacers: "Forgive me, but when you…I have the thought that…"
- Sort projections from perceptions by asking questions.
- If you don't know how to say something in skills, frame it in words or a literal air drawing of a frame.
- Focus on **your** part. Do not use thoughts or statements that begin with the word YOU. If someone offends you, figure out what your part is before complaining.
- Respond to issues or Stage Twos with "Oops," or "I am sorry." Or "I'm sorry, what can I do to make it better?" "I'm sorry. I will take a look at that." "I'm sorry for hurting you, but this is my path."
- No blaming or judging ever. Prepare to be scorned for blaming or judging repeatedly. Mirroring is allowed (use statements starting with "You seem…"). Feelings are also allowed.
- No advice-giving unless you are asked or you are a Master Teacher.
- Avoid presenting a thought or judgment as a feeling. ("I feel **that**…" is wrong.)
- Mirroring is about how someone seems in the moment, not who they are. It must be objective, impartial and unloaded. Use feedback to see how you are coming across, not who you are.
- Be careful not to confuse feedback with a definition of you.

Standards and Values

- Assessing is allowed and expected. (Assessing sees the person's behavior is something they could change. Judging sees their character as inborn.)
- No enabling. If you accept or enable bad behavior, you are a co-conspirator.
- No projecting. If you have a projection, frame it and ask about it.
- No old mirrors allowed. People can change on a dime, so only mention patterns that still exist.
- Never demand. Always use "Would you…?" "Could you…?" Or "Please…."
- Keep your word. If you need to break your word, notify the person first that you are breaking your agreement, and give your true reasons why.
- Don't do evil. Don't scapegoat. Don't harm someone else for your own end.
- Don't make choices, even romantic choices, out of feelings unless the choice is also correct or ethical.
- Do the right thing, even when it's hard, when it is in front of you to do.
- Act with courage, honor, love of truth, and self-observation.
- When you own something and go through the eye of the needle (dropping your ego, going to six o'clock, and owning your original injuries), you heal and change then and there, earning the respect of everyone beholding.
- Love the truth. Speak it as clearly and kindly as possible, unless it will do harm (something you need to learn to assess for yourself).

Group Etiquette

- You may discuss lessons and stories from group, but not names.
- No secrets will be harbored within the group from anyone else in the group, and no relevant issues will be hidden in the family.
- Don't misuse theory to bully in an argument.
- We get to talk about you in your absence, in skills.

Terminating Relationships

- We don't stay in a relationship with people who do evil things.
- It may be harmful to stay in relationship with someone who doesn't use relationship skills.
- Don't terminate a relationship by withdrawing without dialogue.
- Never say "No." Rather say, "Yes, if…"
- Before quitting a relationship cleanly, at least three times tell a person how you feel, how they seem, and what you need.
- Never terminate a relationship in the middle of an issue. Never introduce new reasons for terminating a relationship that have not already been processed or discussed in an agreement or disagreement.
- Don't terminate by devaluing the other person, but you can assess and mirror their choices.
- If you want to terminate, go to the person calmly or come to RSW to give reasons and hear feedback openly. Tell the person or the group what it has been like for you. (Those who terminate group must bring it up in the beginning of group or the meeting, so people have time to react.)
- After terminating, you may stay for your last RSW or leave. Staying or leaving is decided on a case-by-case basis.

Agreement

You are hereby advised you are required to understand The Theory and the Skills Guidelines before participating. By participating, you agree to the rules and guidelines of The Theory, the Relationship Skills Workshops, and you accept correction until you finally practice The Theory as a lifestyle, at which time you may terminate with honor. If you terminate before then, you may seek Honorable Leave Taking, in which you receive the blessings of your RSW members and facilitator. You understand you may not terminate in the middle of an issue. That will not be Honorable Leave Taking, and you may expect those who have committed to this process will not give you comfort for doing so because to do so would also be dishonorable.

Cameras and Videotaping

PaRC is an educational facility. While we want to help as many students and clients as possible, we also want to train as many therapists as possible, especially before Dr. Faye passes on the baton. We anticipate recording students under certain and special circumstances for these purposes. As you will notice there are video cameras on the premises. These cameras loop. After approximately three weeks they record over previous material. No material will be reviewed unless one of five reasons develops. Our taping is for the following specific purposes only:

(1) We leave the doors unlocked so no one will ever be locked out. With video surveillance we will be able to identify anyone who has stolen anything from the premises or anyone who has destroyed property.

(2) On occasion someone acts out in a very dramatic way and has no idea how they are shooting themselves in the foot. On such occasions it is extremely helpful to be able to pull the specific and limited footage off the recorder onto a memory stick so the student can see himself or herself. This can be a powerful wake-up tool. In this case the only person to see the footage will be the subject. If there are other people in view, then they will have to review the footage in our office on the tape deck, and no copy will be provided, unless the other parties sign a release.

(3) On occasion there is a disagreement as to what someone did or said, and it may work well to be able to find and review the moment in question. If the dispute involves more than one person, those involved will be allowed to review the footage. It will automatically be erased when the loop is complete, and the recording will continue over the previous footage.

(4) On occasion couchworks or private sessions may be classically ideal to provide examples of how the Snyder Causal Therapy Treatment process works and how effective it is. If a client experiences just such a couchwork, we may ask if they are willing to let us use that couchwork for training or educational purposes. In this case we will offer to disguise their face and voice. The client may refuse to allow us to use the footage, or they may wish to review it and decide how much they are willing to share, if at all.

(5) PaRC has plans at some point to offer our services for free or low cost to subjects who would be willing to participate in a documentary or educational program that follows ten to twelve students from beginning to termination. We will be using these edited sessions to demonstrate for therapists across the country how our technique works. If a distributor wants to pick us up, we will consider it. All students involved in this program will have rights that will be reviewed specifically with the participants when the time comes.

No video tape will be used to otherwise violate a person's privacy and confidentiality.

Telemedicine

You understand "telemedicine" includes the practice of health care delivery, diagnosis, consultation, treatment, transfer of medical data, and education using interactive audio, video, and/or data communications. You understand telemedicine also involves the communication of your medical/mental information, both orally and visually, to health care practitioners located in or out of California. You understand this is only an adjunct to your regular therapy, and if it becomes too protracted you will be billed. You understand you have the following rights with respect to telemedicine:

- You have the right to withhold or withdraw consent at any time without affecting your right to future care or treatment, nor risking the loss or withdrawal of any program benefits to which you would otherwise be entitled.
- The laws that protect the confidentiality of your medical information also apply to telemedicine. As such, you understand the information disclosed by you during the course of your therapy is generally confidential. However, there are both mandatory and permissive exceptions to confidentiality, including, but not limited to reporting child, elder, and dependent adult abuse; expressed threats of suicide or violence towards an ascertainable victim; and where you make your mental or emotional state an issue in a legal proceeding.
- You have read the section herein on Confidentiality and Secrecy.
- If you are in RSW you understand any information from your participation may be discussed about you while you are absent or written about you to the facilitator.
- You will not divulge the names of any persons in your group along with any information learned about them while in the context of our RSW, including emails shared in group. Emails related to you may be shared with them for therapeutic purposes and to update them on a process. If you terminate in the middle of an issue by email, that information may be shared with the group as well.
- If you are involved in a relationship with anyone else doing Causal Therapy as a couple, as a family, or within an RSW, email transmissions about them may be shared with them by our mutual facilitator.
- My therapist reserves the right to withhold treatment if you do not agree to the above three items because she or he believes withholding secrets in a relationship is commonly anti-therapeutic, and her therapeutic goal for you, generally speaking, is to live life enjoying privacy but without secrecy.
- You also understand the dissemination of any personally identifiable images or information from the telemedicine interaction to researchers or other entities, with the exception of people with whom you are in a therapeutic relationship, as described above, shall not occur without your written consent.
- You understand there are risks and consequences from telemedicine, including but not limited to, the possibility despite reasonable efforts on the part of your psychotherapist: the transmission of your medical information could be disrupted or distorted by technical failures; the transmission of your medical information could be interrupted by unauthorized persons; and/or the electronic storage of your medical information could be accessed by unauthorized persons.
- In addition, you understand telemedicine-based services and care may not be as complete as face-to-face services. You also understand if your psychotherapist believes you would be better served by another form of psychotherapeutic services (e.g. face-to-face services) you will ask to table the discussion until you are in the recommended venue. Finally, you understand there are potential risks and benefits associated with any form of psychotherapy, and despite your efforts and the efforts of your psychotherapist, your condition may not improve, and in some cases may even get worse. When you suspect this is the case, you will bring it up in therapy.
- You understand you may benefit from telemedicine, but results cannot be guaranteed or assured.
- You understand you have a right to access your medical information and copies of medical records in accordance with California law.
- You agree to give a 24-hour cancellation notice to your therapist in order not to be billed for a scheduled session either in person, by telephone, or by email.
- If you have any questions about this policy, you will discuss them with your therapist.

HIPAA/Notice of Privacy Practices

This notice describes how medical information about you may be used and disclosed, and you can access this information. Please review it carefully.

I. I HAVE A LEGAL DUTY TO SAFEGUARD YOUR PROTECTED HEALTH INFORMATION (PHI). I am legally required to protect the privacy of your PHI, which includes information that can be used to identify you that I've created or received about your past, present, or future health or condition, the provision of health care to you, or the payment of this health care. I must provide you with this Notice about my privacy practices, and such Notice must explain how, when, and why I will "use" and "disclose" your PHI. A "use" of PHI occurs when I share, examine, utilize, apply, or analyze such information within my practice; PHI is "disclosed" when it is released, transferred, has been given to, or is otherwise divulged to a third party outside of my practice. With some exceptions, I may not use or disclose any more of your PHI than is necessary to accomplish the purpose for which the use or disclosure is made. And, I am legally required to follow the privacy practices described in this Notice. However, I reserve the right to change the terms of this Notice and my privacy policies at any time. Any changes will apply to PHI on file with me already. Before I make any important changes to my policies, I will promptly change this Notice and post a new copy of it in my office. You can also request a copy of this Notice from me.

II. HOW I MAY USE AND DISCLOSE YOUR PHI. I will use and disclose your PHI for many different reasons. For some of these uses or disclosures, I will need your prior authorization; for others, however, I do not. Listed below are the different categories of my uses and disclosures along with some examples of each category.

   A. Uses and disclosures specifically relating to treatment, payment, or health care operations do not require your prior written consent. I can use and disclose your PHI without your consent for the following reasons:

      1. For treatment. I can disclose your PHI to physicians, psychiatrists, psychologists, and other licensed health care providers who provide you with health care services or are involved in your care. For example, if you're being treated by a psychiatrist, I can disclose your PHI to your psychiatrist in order to coordinate your care.

      2. To obtain payment for treatment. I can use and disclose your PHI to bill and collect payment for the treatment and services provided by me to you. For example, I might send your PHI to your insurance company or health plan to get paid for the health care services I have provided to you. I may also provide your PHI to my business associates, such as billing companies, claims processing companies, and others that process my health care claims.

      3. For health care operations. I can disclose your PHI to operate my practice. For example, I might use your PHI to evaluate the quality of health care services you received or to evaluate the performance of the health care professionals who provided such services to you. I may also provide your PHI to our accountants, attorneys, consultants, and others to make sure I'm com-plying with applicable laws.

      4. Other disclosures. I may also disclose your PHI to others without your consent in certain situations. For example, your consent isn't required if you need emergency treatment, as long as I try to get your consent after treatment is rendered, or if I try to get your consent but you are unable to communicate with me (for example, if you are unconscious or in severe pain) and I think you would consent to such treatment if you were able to do so.

   B. Certain other uses and disclosures do not require your consent. I can use and disclose your PHI without your consent or authorization for the following reasons:

      1. When disclosure is required by federal, state or local law; judicial or administrative proceedings; or law enforcement. For example, I may make a disclosure to applicable officials when a law requires me to report information to government agencies and law enforcement personnel about victims of abuse or neglect; or when ordered in a judicial or administrative proceeding.

      2. For public health activities. For example, I may have to report information about you to the county coroner.

      3. For health oversight activities. For example, I may have to provide information to assist the government when it conducts an investigation or inspection of a health care provider or organization.

4. For research purposes. In certain circumstances, I may provide PHI in order to conduct medical research.
5. To avoid harm. In order to avoid a serious threat to the PHI to law enforcement personnel or persons able to prevent or lessen such harm.
6. For specific government functions. I may disclose PHI of military personnel and veterans in certain situations. And I may disclose PHI for national security purposes, such as protecting the President of the United States or conducting intelligence operations.
7. For workers' compensation purposes. I may provide PHI in order to comply with workers' compensation laws.
8. Appointment reminders and health related benefits or services. I may use PHI to provide appointment reminders or give you information about treatment alternatives, or other health care services or benefits I offer.

C. Certain uses and disclosures require you to have the opportunity to object. Disclosures to family, friends, or others. I may provide your PHI to a family member, friend, or other person that you indicate is involved in your care or the payment for your health care, unless you object in whole or in part. The opportunity to consent may be obtained retroactively in emergency situations.

D. Other uses and disclosures require your prior written authorization. In any other situation not described in sections A, B, and C above, I will ask for your written authorization before using or disclosing any of your PHI. If you choose to sign an authorization to disclose your PHI, you can later revoke such authorization in writing to stop any further authorization.

III. YOUR RIGHTS REGARDING YOUR PHI. You have the following rights with respect to your PHI:

A. The Right to Request Limits on Uses and Disclosures of Your PHI. You have the right to ask I limit how I use and disclose your PHI. I will consider your request, but I am not legally required to accept it. If I accept your request, I will put any limits in writing and abide by them except in emergency situations. You may not limit the uses and disclosures I am legally required or allowed to make.

B. The Right to Choose How I Send PHI to You. You have the right to ask I send information to you to at an alternate address (for example, sending information to your work address rather than your home address) or by alternate means (for example, e-mail instead of regular mail) I must agree to your request so long as I can easily provide the PHI to you in the format you requested.

C. The Right to See and Get Copies of Your PHI. In most cases, you have the right to look at or get copies of your PHI that I have, but you must make the request in writing. If I don't have your PHI but I know who does, I will tell you how to get it. I will respond to you within 30 days of receiving your written request. In certain situations, I may deny your request. If I do, I will tell you, in writing, my reasons for the denial and explain your right to have my denial reviewed. If you request copies of your PHI, I will charge you not more than $.25 for each page. Instead of providing the PHI you requested, I may provide you with a summary or explanation of the PHI as long as you agree to that and to the cost in advance.

D. The Right to Get a List of the Disclosures I Have Made. You have the right to get a list of instances in which I have disclosed your PHI. The list will not include uses or disclosures you have already consented to, such as those made for treatment, payment, or health care operations, directly to you, or to your family. The list also won't include uses and disclosures made for national security purposes, to corrections or law enforcement personnel, or disclosures made before April 15, 2003. I will respond to your request for an accounting of disclosures within 60 days of receiving your request. The list I will give you will include disclosures made in the last six years unless you request a shorter time. The list will include the date of the disclosure, to whom PHI was disclosed (including their address, if known), a description of the information disclosed, and the reason for the disclosure. I will provide the list to you at no charge, but if you make more than one request in the same year, I will charge you a reasonable cost-based fee for each additional request.

E. The Right to Correct or Update Your PHI. If you believe there is a mistake in your PHI or a piece of important information is missing, you have the right to request I correct the existing information or add missing information. You must provide the request and your reason for the request in writing. I will respondwithin 60 days of receiving your request to correct or update your PHI. I may deny your request in writing if the PHI is (i) correct and complete, (ii) not created by me, (iii) not allowed to be disclosed, or (iv) not part of my records. My written denial will state the reasons for the denial and explain your right to file a written state-ment of disagreement with the denial. If you don't file one, you have the right to request your request and my denial be attached to all future disclosures of your PHI. If I approve your request, I will make the changeto your PHI, tell you I have done it, and tell others need to know about the change to your PHI.

    F. The Right to Get This Notice by E-Mail. You have the right to get a copy of this notice by e-mail. Even if you have agreed to receive notice via email, you also have the right to request a paper copy of it.

IV. HOW TO COMPLAIN ABOUT MY PRIVACY PRACTICES. If you think I may have violated your privacy rights, or you disagree with a decision I made about access to your PHI, you may file a complaint with the person listed in Section VI below. You also may send a written complaint to the Secretary of the Department of Health and Human Services at 200 Independence Avenue S.W., Washington, D.C. 20201. I will take no retaliatory action against you if you file a complaint about my privacy practices.

V. PERSON TO CONTACT FOR INFORMATION ABOUT THIS NOTICE OR TO COMPLAIN ABOUT MY PRIVACY PRACTICES.If you have any questions about this notice or any complaints about my privacy practices you could discuss it with your therapist.

VI. EFFECTIVE DATE OF THIS NOTICE. This notice went into effect on April 14, 2003.

You have been advised of the HIPPA/Notice of Privacy Practices.

Signature Page (Client Copy)

Printed Name: ____

Please initial before every statement to signify agreement. This page intended for your file reference.

_______ I understand if my therapist is an intern, she or he will be sharing the progress of my/our case with his/her supervisor and cohorts in Group Supervision. If my partner and I are in couples counseling with separate therapists, I understand and release my therapist to consult with the other therapist.

_______ If it is relevant for my therapist to consult with a previous therapist and/or doctor, I hereby release my therapist to make contact with that provider. Email: _______________________________________ Phone: ___________________

_______ I understand if I am doing therapy with a partner, I may not ask my therapist to keep a secret from my partner. I have the choice of revealing that information to my partner before going forward, or my therapist will need to terminate therapy because keeping a secret from the couple is not good for the couple or the other party. However, if the secret is irrelevant and would be harmful to the couple if shared, then the therapist may make this secret an exception after a discussion.

_______ If I am in a custody dispute, I agree to minimize conflict for my child(ren)'s sake.

_______ I have studied the Causal Theory in one way or another: Live class, online, DVDs or CDs, *The Manual*, *The Handbook* or *Co-parenting: Healing in the Courts*. I have received PaRC's booklet, *The Way of PaRC*, and will have read it before beginning my work at PaRC.

_______ I understand and agree to PaRC's goals of openness and authenticity where they are healthy, realistic and applicable.

_______ I agree not to use names outside of PaRC/RSW and if I do, I understand I may be asked to leave.

_______ I agree not to blame others, but I am allowed to briefly explain my history, thinking and circumstances to create understanding. If I break this agreement, I expect to be confronted and possibly "arrested" (stopped from blaming). If correction is embarrassing, hopefully that will be a deterrent to further blaming in the future. In other words, if I blame, I will be corrected. That's the contract.

_______ I agree never to quit this relationship or any relationship without attempting at least three times to respectfully communicate my issue before leaving.

_______ If I need to complain, I will offer feedback to the administrator at PaRC and attempt to have my issue mediated by a veteran of my choosing at PaRC.

_______ I agree to the Therapy Contract previously described, specifically that I have vetted my therapist and facilitator(s) and now unconditionally and without debate take my therapist and facilitator as my teacher(s). If I cannot do that, we agree to part amicably.

_______ I accept the facilitator of any group I join at PaRC as my teacher.

_______ I will not offer advice or "should" on anyone else.

_______ During any time in private therapy, I agree to PaRC's Therapeutic Goals and understand I may add further goals at any time.

_______ I have been informed PaRC is an educational facility, and I understand how and whether the cameras will affect me, including my rights to confidentiality.

_______ I have read and understand HIPPA/Notice of Privacy Practices. I understand I am entitled to confidentiality with the exceptions of child, elder and dependent person's abuse or if there is a potential plan to injure someone specific.

Signature: ____ Date: ___________________

Signature Page (For Therapist)

Printed Name: ____

Please initial before every statement to signify agreement, sign it at the bottom, then tear it out and give it to your therapist.

______ I understand if my therapist is an intern, she or he will be sharing the progress of my/our case with his/her supervisor and cohorts in Group Supervision. If my partner and I are in couples counseling with separate therapists, I understand and release my therapist to consult with the other therapist.

______ If it is relevant for my therapist to consult with a previous therapist and/or doctor, I hereby release my therapist to make contact with that provider. Email: ____ Phone: ____________________________

______ I understand if I am doing therapy with a partner, I may not ask my therapist to keep a secret from my partner. I have the choice of revealing that information to my partner before going forward, or my therapist will need to terminate therapy because keeping a secret from the couple is not good for the couple or the other party. However, if the secret is irrelevant and would be harmful to the couple if shared, then the therapist may make this secret an exception after a discussion.

______ If I am in a custody dispute, I agree to minimize conflict for my child(ren)'s sake.

______ I have studied the Causal Theory in one way or another: Live class, online, DVDs or CDs, *The Manual*, *The Handbook* or *Co-parenting: Healing in the Courts*. I have received PaRC's booklet, *The Way of PaRC*, and will have read it before beginning my work at PaRC.

______ I understand and agree to PaRC's goals of openness and authenticity where they are healthy, realistic and applicable.

______ I agree not to use names outside of PaRC/RSW and if I do, I understand I may be asked to leave.

______ I agree not to blame others, but I am allowed to briefly explain my history, thinking and circumstances to create understanding. If I break this agreement, I expect to be confronted and possibly "arrested" (stopped from blaming). If correction is embarrassing, hopefully that will be a deterrent to further blaming in the future. In other words, if I blame, I will be corrected. That's the contract.

______ I agree never to quit this relationship or any relationship without attempting at least three times to respectfully communicate my issue before leaving.

______ If I need to complain, I will offer feedback to the administrator at PaRC and attempt to have my issue mediated by a veteran of my choosing at PaRC.

______ I agree to the Therapy Contract previously described, specifically that I have vetted my therapist and facilitator(s) and now unconditionally and without debate take my therapist and facilitator as my teacher(s). If I cannot do that, we agree to part amicably.

______ I accept the facilitator of any group I join at PaRC as my teacher.

______ I will not offer advice or "should" on anyone else.

______ During any time in private therapy, I agree to PaRC's Therapeutic Goals and understand I may add further goals at any time.

______ I have been informed PaRC is an educational facility, and I understand how and whether the cameras will affect me, including my rights to confidentiality.

______ I have read and understand HIPPA/Notice of Privacy Practices. I understand I am entitled to confidentiality with the exceptions of child, elder and dependent person's abuse or if there is a potential plan to injure someone specific.

Signature: ____ Date: ____________________